THE GREAT GATSBY

The Limits of Wonder

TWAYNE'S MASTERWORK STUDIES
ROBERT LECKER, GENERAL EDITOR

THE GREAT GATSBY

The Limits of Wonder

Richard Lehan

TWAYNE PUBLISHERS

NEW YORK

PRENTICE HALL INTERNATIONAL

LONDON · MEXICO CITY · NEW DELHI · SINGAPORE · SYDNEY · TORONTO

Twayne's Masterwork Studies No. 36

Twayne Publishers

1633 Broadway, New York, NY 10019-6785
New York, NY 10022

Copyediting supervised by Barbara Sutton.
Book production by Janet Z. Reynolds.
Typeset by Compositors Corp., Cedar Rapids, Iowa.

Printed on permanent/durable acid-free paper
and bound in the United States of America.

Library of Congress Cataloging in Publication Data
Lehan, Richard Daniel, 1930–
    The great Gatsby : the limits of wonder / Richard Lehan.
        p.   cm. — (Twayne's masterwork studies ; no 36)
    Bibliography: p.
    Includes index.
    ISBN 0-8057-7960-4 (alk. paper). — ISBN 0-8057-8013-0 (pbk. :
alk. paper)
    1. Fitzgerald, F. Scott (Francis Scott), 1896–1940. Great Gatsby.
I. Title. II. Series.
PS3511.I9G854   1990
813'.52—dc20   89-15484
                                                            CIP

To my students at
    the University of Wisconsin 1953–57,
    the University of Texas 1958–62,
    and UCLA 1962 to the present,
who for over three decades have shared my enthusiasm
for this wonderful novel.

... gradually I became aware of the old island here that flowered once for Dutch sailors' eyes—a fresh green breast of the new world. Its vanished trees ... had once pandered in whispers to the last and greatest of all human dreams; for a transitory enchanted moment man must have held his breath in the presence of this continent, compelled into an aesthetic contemplation he neither understood nor desired, face to face for the last time in history with something commensurate to his capacity for wonder.

—F. Scott Fitzgerald, *The Great Gatsby*

CONTENTS

NOTE ON THE REFERENCES
AND ACKNOWLEDGMENTS

I am concerned in this study with supplying a context that will explain F. Scott Fitzgerald's *The Great Gatsby* as both a product of the twenties and as a living work of art that still speaks to us in a vital way. Over the past forty years my own response to this novel has changed many times, but my admiration and awe at Fitzgerald's achievement have never altered. In this reading, I have emphasized how much Fitzgerald owed to a romantic sense of history, which he then applied to the story of America. Such a context has helped explain for me a great deal of what leads to the complexity of this deceivingly simple and sad story. In the last several decades, I have learned much from Fitzgerald's able critics, whose yeoman work I have tried to acknowledge herein. I am also immensely grateful to almost two generations of students, who have shared my enthusiasm for Fitzgerald and who have helped make the reading of *Gatsby* such a living and relevant experience. More immediately, I should like to thank Joan M. Corbette and Melanie Eckford-Prossor for their typing, Chris Mott for his legwork in the library, and Robert Metzger for help with proofreading. Most of all, my thanks to Ann and Teddy, who were there when I most needed them.

I have used the Scribner's edition of *The Great Gatsby*, quotations reprinted with permission of Charles Scribner's Sons, an imprint of Macmillan Publishing Company, Copyright 1925 by Charles Scribner's Sons; copyright renewed 1953 by Frances Scott Fitzgerald Lanahan.

F. Scott Fitzgerald in the late 1930s at the Algonquin Hotel in New York.

CHRONOLOGY:
F. Scott Fitzgerald's Life and Works

1890	Edward Fitzgerald and Mollie Quillan marry on 12 February. Mollie is the oldest daughter of Philip F. McQuillan, who was born in Ireland and settled in Galena, Illinois, before he moved to St. Paul in 1859, where he prospered in the wholesale grocery business. Edward Fitzgerald was the son of Michael Fitzgerald from Maryland, who married Cecilia Ashton Scott, making Francis Scott Fitzgerald a distant cousin of Francis Scott Key.
1896	Fitzgerald born on Laurel Avenue in St. Paul.
1898	Edward Fitzgerald moves family to Buffalo where he works as a salesman for Procter & Gamble.
1901	Family moves to Syracuse in January.
1903	Moves back to Buffalo in September.
1908	Edward Fitzgerald loses his job with Procter & Gamble and moves back to St. Paul.
1911	Fitzgerald enters Newman School, Hackensack, New Jersey, where he meets Father Cyril Sigourney Webster Fay, who will have an important early intellectual influence on him.
1912	Meets Shane Leslie through Father Fay in November.
1913	Enters Princeton University in September; becomes friends with Edmund Wilson and John Peale Bishop.
1914	Meets Ginevra King in St. Paul in December.
1915	Dates Ginevra King throughout the year. They attend a New York dinner dance in January and a play and the Follies in June.
1916	Returns to Princeton in September after having dropped out his junior year. Ginevra is expelled from Westover finishing school in March. Visits Ginevra in Lake Forest, Illinois, in August.
1917	Breaks with Ginevra in January. Ginevra is engaged in June. Fitzgerald leaves Princeton in October to accept a 2d lieutenant

commission in the infantry. Sent to Fort Leavenworth where he begins "The Romantic Egoist."

1918   Transferred to Camp Taylor, Louisville, Kentucky, in February; to Camp Gordon, Georgia, in April; and to Camp Sheridan outside of Montgomery, Alabama, in June. Learns in June that Ginevra is to be married 24 September. Meets Zelda Sayre in July. Scribner's declines his novel in August as well as a revised submission in October. Is sent to Camp Mills, New York, in November, but war ends before he is sent overseas.

1919   Discharged from the army, goes to New York where he works for the Barron Collier advertising agency. Leaves New York in July for St. Paul, where he rewrites his novel that summer. Resubmits novel to Scribner's, which accepts it in September.

1920   Returns to the South in January and is engaged to Zelda. Publishes "The Ice Palace" among other short stories. *This Side of Paradise* published 26 March. Marries Zelda in the rectory of St. Patrick's Cathedral, New York, 3 April. After honeymoon, they live in Westport, Connecticut. Publishes "May Day" in the *Smart Set* and *Flappers and Philosophers* in the autumn.

1921   The Fitzgeralds leave for Europe in May, return in July. Spend rest of the summer in White Bear Lake, Minnesota. Daughter born in October. They live in St. Paul from November to June 1922.

1922   *The Beautiful and Damned* published in March; "The Diamond as Big as the Ritz" published in June issue of the *Smart Set*. In the summer they move to White Bear Yacht Club, where Fitzgerald conceptualizes an early version of *The Great Gatsby*. *Tales of the Jazz Age* published in September. Fitzgeralds move back to New York where they live at 6 Gateway Drive, Great Neck. Here they meet Ring Lardner and come to know the world that will serve as the setting of *The Great Gatsby*. "Winter Dreams" published in the December issue of *Metropolitan*.

1923   Fitzgerald's play, *The Vegetable*, fails in Atlantic City in November, after which he turns for five months to short story writing to pay off debts.

1924   Fitzgeralds leave in May for Europe for what will be a protracted stay. Eventually settle in St. Raphaël on the Riviera and meet Gerald and Sara Murphy at Cap d'Antibes. This experience will be central to the plot of *Tender Is the Night*. "Absolution" published in June issue of *American Mercury*. From summer through to the fall, Fitzgerald writes a first draft of *The Great*

Gatsby. Moves in the winter to Rome, where he revises *The Great Gatsby.*

1925   Fitzgeralds move to Capri in February, return to Paris in the spring, where they meet Ernest Hemingway. *The Great Gatsby* published on 10 April.

1926   Publication of "The Rich Boy" in *Redbook* in January, and publication of *All the Sad Young Men* in February. Family spends spring and summer once again on the Riviera before returning home in December.

1927   Fitzgerald goes to Hollywood, where he works for United Artists and meets Lois Moran, who will become the model for Rosemary Hoyt in *Tender Is the Night.* Family settles in Ellerslie, a mansion outside of Wilmington, Delaware, in March.

1928   Leave for Europe in April and remain until September, when they again settle at Ellerslie.

1929   Return to Europe in March. Publication of "The Last of the Belles" in the *Saturday Evening Post.*

1930   Zelda experiences her first mental breakdown in April. In June, family moves to Switzerland where she enters the Prangens clinic.

1931   Fitzgerald's father dies in January. Publication of "Babylon Revisited" in February issue of the *Saturday Evening Post.* Return to America in September. Zelda lives with parents while Fitzgerald goes to Hollywood to work for Metro-Goldwyn-Mayer.

1932   Zelda suffers second breakdown in February, is hospitalized in Baltimore. Fitzgerald lives at La Paix, outside city, where Zelda joins him in June.

1933   Move to house on Park Avenue in Baltimore.

1934   Zelda suffers third breakdown in January. *Tender Is the Night* published in April.

1935   Fitzgerald ill, goes in February to Tyron, North Carolina, for a rest. *Taps at Reveille* published in March. Spends summer in Asheville, North Carolina; moves back to Baltimore in the fall and then to Hendersonville, North Carolina, for the winter. Begins writing *The Crack-Up* essays.

1936   Zelda institutionalized in April in Highland Hospital, Asheville. Fitzgerald's mother dies in September.

1937   Fitzgerald goes to Hollywood for the third time in July to accept a six-month contract with MGM. Meets Sheilah Graham during the summer.

1938 Moves in April from the Garden of Allah to Malibu Colony, and in October from Malibu to Encino where he lives in a cottage on the estate of Edward Everett Horton. MGM contract not renewed in December.

1939 During trip to Dartmouth College to work on Walter Wanger film, *Winter Carnival*, Fitzgerald goes on a drunken spree—ends up in New York hospital. Free-lances in Hollywood from spring to fall of 1940.

1940 Working on *The Last Tycoon*, publishing the "Pat Hobby" stories in *Esquire*. Moves in May to North Laurel Avenue, Hollywood. Dies of a heart attack on 21 December and buried in Rockville Union Cemetery on 27 December.

1941 Publication in October of the incomplete *The Last Tycoon*.

1945 Publication of *The Crack-Up* in August.

1948 Zelda burned to death in a fire at Highland Hospital.

1

Historical Context

GATSBY'S AMERICA

On 2 April 1917 President Woodrow Wilson went before Congress asking for a declaration of war against the Central Powers; on 11 November 1918—on the eleventh hour of the eleventh day of the eleventh month—the Armistice ending World War I went into effect. During that time 4,335,000 American men had been mobilized for war and 364,000 of them had died. As tragic as those figures may be, they are eclipsed by the fact that the allies—Britain, France, Russia, and Italy—mobilized almost thirty-five million men, twenty-one million of whom died in the war. The Central Powers—mainly Germany and Austria—had mobilized twenty-three million men, fifteen million of whom became casualties. The human cost for rearranging the map of the Balkans was enormous; and after the Armistice many, rightly it would turn out, felt that the war had done little more than plant the seeds for another war.

F. Scott Fitzgerald suggested as much in his first novel, *This Side of Paradise*, a study in the disillusioning belief that World War I would be the war to end all wars. And yet Fitzgerald was sorely disappointed that he did not get to serve overseas. He identified with the collective experiences of his generation and felt that he had been left out of the major event. Whatever experience he may have missed, he made up for after the war, and there is probably no writer who is more identified with a decade than Fitzgerald is identified with the 1920s. His short stories defined the flapper and the new morality, and his novels caught the essence of the historical moment. While *The Great Gatsby* suggests rather than develops the era of the twenties, it does evoke a haunting mood of a glamorous, wild time that seemingly will never come again. The loss of an ideal, the disillusionment that comes with the failure to compromise, the efforts of runaway prosperity and wild parties, the fear of the intangibility of that moment, the built-in resentment against the new immigration, the fear of a new radical element, the latent racism behind half-baked historical theories, the effect of Prohibition, the rise of a powerful underworld, the effect of the automobile and professional sports on postwar America—these and a dozen equally important events became the subject of *The Great Gatsby*, a novel that evokes both the romance and the sadness of that strange and fascinating era we call the twenties.

The major events of the era were laid down after the Franco-Prussian war in 1870–71. At that time Chancellor Otto von Bismarck juggled Germany, Russia, and Austria in a triple alliance known as the Three Emperors' League. But as Germany and Austria moved closer politically, Russia was discarded by Kaiser Wilhelm II in 1888. When this happened, Russia and France formed their own alliance, England later joining them, which arranged the major powers of Europe into two potentially hostile camps. What made it more dangerous was the political instability of the dual monarchy of the Austro-Hungarian Empire, ruled over by the House of Hapsburg. The fatal moment came with the assassination of Archduke Francis Ferdinand and his wife on 28 June 1914. Austria held Serbia responsible for this terrorist act and declared war on 28 July. Russia came to the aid of Serbia, and on 31 October Germany responded to Russia's mobilization with an ultimatum of its own, which brought France and later England into the fray on the side of Russia—and World War I was under way.

Woodrow Wilson had run for a second term in 1916 on the grounds that he had kept America out of the war, and yet almost the first thing he did after assuming a new term as president was to declare war on the Central Powers. While American generals like Pershing welcomed participation in the war, they also felt that they were playing a secondary role to the other major powers, especially the British and the French. And what was true of Pershing during the war was even more true of Wilson during the peace process, where he found himself totally outmaneuvered by Lloyd George of England, Georges Clemenceau of France, and Vittorio Orlando of Italy. Despite his own initial reservations about the Versailles Treaty, Wilson eventually gave total consent to this peace treaty, idealized it beyond a willingness to allow compromise, and brought it to the American public in an address to the Senate on 10 July 1919. Despite Wilson's support the treaty was doomed to failure, primarily because it contained the idea of the League of Nations with the provision that members of the League would protect "the territorial integrity and existing political independence of all members of the League." Led by Senator Henry Cabot Lodge of Massachusetts, many in Congress felt that this was an invitation to get America involved in another European war, and they managed to defeat the treaty in the Congress. Unwilling to compromise his ideals in any way, the undaunted Wilson took his fight to the people, and on 3 September 1919 began a coast-to-coast train trip. As the trip progressed, the strain began to show on Wilson who, nevertheless, plunged on in the face of ill health and exhaustion, until he suffered a stroke on 25 September outside of Pueblo, Colorado. For over a year and a half, until his term ran out, the Wilson presidency was more or less run by his wife and several aides. The country witnessed a man with unbending ideals going down to a bitter defeat, emptied of his vitality in the process. The Wilson experience has its counterpart in *The Great Gatsby*, a novel that plays directly upon the theme of the defeated idealist, the spirit of which is embodied in the novel by a man named Wilson, with the additional presidential name of George.

The Great Gatsby is a novel that is set against the ending of the war. Both Nick and Gatsby have participated in the war, although like much of the historical background in the novel, these events are more implied than developed. When Nick first meets Gatsby, Gatsby asks, "Your face is familiar. . . . Weren't you in the Third Division during the war?" Nick tells him "Yes . . . . the ninth machine-gun battalion," to which Gatsby responds, "I was in the Seventh Infantry until June nineteen eighteen."[1] Later we are told that Gatsby "did extraordinarily well in the war. He was a captain before he went to the front, and following the Argonne battles he got his majority and the command of the divisional machine-guns" (150). In the first printing of the novel Fitzgerald had Gatsby and Nick in the First, not the Third Division. In subsequent editions their fighting takes place in the Third Division, but what unit Gatsby served in after June 1918 is left unstated, although clearly he fought in the Argonne.

To understand what is going on here it is necessary to know that there were two major battles in 1918, one in the spring, the other in the fall. In the spring the Germans took the offensive, reaching the Marne River and seizing a small bridgehead around Chateau-Thierry, where they ran into the Americans. At this time the First Division had been sent up to the Somme where they engaged the Germans, while the Third Division held the Marne crossing around Chateau-Thierry until the Germans finally abandoned the offensive on 19 July. The allies' counterattack came in the fall. The first battle began as a pincer movement south to cut off the Germans. It was a Franco-American affair, launched on 26 September and known as the Battle of the Meuse-Argonne; it involved the Americans in the hardest fighting of the war, which is probably why Fitzgerald used it in his novel. The eastern boundary of the attack was the Heights of Meuse, where the French and Germans had fought murderously two years before. Westward, the front line crossed the valley of the Meuse, climbed some more hills into the valley of the Aire River, and then ran to the Argonne Forest, roughly one hundred square miles of wood. At 5:25 A.M. on 4 October 1918, Pershing's 32d and Third Divisions attacked the heights northwest of Romagne, and the 77th, 28th, and First Divisions moved on the formidable Argonne bluffs and the ridges north of Exermont. Thus the only way to reconcile the facts of the novel with the facts of history is to assume that Gatsby fought with the Third Division at the Battle of the Marne until June and then with the First Division at Argonne from September to November 1918. The Meuse-Argonne campaign was the last great battle in the American effort. More than a million Americans were involved, many seeing action for the first time, and it involved their bloodiest fighting. In 1926 the War Department released the most accurate battle figures—26,277 Americans dead and 95,786 wounded.

Fitzgerald could think of the war in heroic terms, just as he would think of some of those who went to the war in terms slightly larger than life. Once the war ended, he could project these romantic feelings onto social figures and athletes. In his copy of André Malraux's novel *Man's Hope* (1938) Fitzgerald would pencil in the impressions that helped him create the social world of Gatsby. He refers, for example, to the Rumsies and the Hitchcocks. Thomas Hitchcock and Charles C. Rumsey were famous polo players on Long Island when Fitzgerald moved to Great Neck in 1922. Hitchcock had learned to play polo on his wealthy parents' estate in Old Westbury. At the age of seventeen Hitchcock had joined the Lafayette Escadrille, a group of American volunteers in the French aviation service. He was shot down in March 1918, imprisoned to Lecheld from which, once he had recovered from a thigh wound, he managed to escape, making his way to freedom in Switzerland. Once he returned to the war, he downed three German planes, received the Croix de Guerre, and came home a hero at the age of eighteen. After the war he was equally famous as a polo player, leading the American team to victory over the British in 1921. Charles Rumsey was also a well-known polo player when Fitzgerald was living on Long Island. From 1913 on he was a member of every United States polo team to compete in international cup matches. Married to Mary Harriman, the daughter of railroad magnate Edward H. Harriman, he was killed on 21 September 1922 when thrown from the car in which he was riding, an event that was much in keeping with the romantic-tragic mood of Fitzgerald's novel.

After the war the American economy went into a slight recession that was followed by an era of almost uninterrupted prosperity culminating with the stock market crash of 1929. For Fitzgerald, the Jazz Age began in 1918 and ended in 1929—dates he would later personalize; his flapper comes into being at the age of eighteen, and the illusions of youth fade at twenty-nine. Even in *The Great Gatsby*, published in 1925, these dates take on a kind of prescient significance: Gatsby and Daisy consummate their love when she is eighteen, and Nick turns thirty the day that

Gatsby's dream dies. These were years of cataclysmic change for the nation. According to the 1920 census, for the first time there were more Americans living in cities than in rural areas. The frontier had long been redefined by Frederick Jackson Turner, a thesis that was given additional attention in the twenties when his collection of essays, *The Frontier in American History*, was published in 1920. Van Wyck Brooks's *The Ordeal of Mark Twain* (1922) reworked some of those ideas, suggesting America was culturally divided between a spirit of the West and of the East. Both the Turner and Brooks theses would be worked into *The Great Gatsby*.

From 1900 to 1920 the number of factory workers in America had doubled, going from 4.7 million to 9 million, with 3 million more working in related manufacturing jobs. Many of these jobs were being filled by the wave of new immigrants, mostly from southern and eastern Europe. There were almost no laws regulating working conditions, and labor unions were extremely weak. Many of the new immigrants brought with them socialist or anarchist ideas from Europe—or so many frightened capitalists argued—and Americans showed growing fear and resentment of "foreigners." On May Day 1919 socialist red-flag parades were broken up in a dozen cities by angry mobs, with three killed and hundreds injured. In New York the offices of the Socialist *Daily Call* were ransacked by off-duty soldiers in uniform. Such raids were encouraged by the vigilante tactics of Attorney General A. Mitchell Palmer. Fitzgerald described these kinds of events in "May Day," and in *The Great Gatsby* he described the streets of New York filling up with people with "the tragic eyes and short upper lips of southeastern Europe," an illusion that gets picked up with Meyer Wolfsheim and his "gonnegtions." Fitzgerald also described blacks coming from the South to cities like Chicago and New York, where by 1920 over three hundred thousand blacks would be living in Harlem. As Gatsby and Nick enter the city over the Queensboro Bridge, they see a panorama of ethnic faces outlined against the skyline of the new city, itself one of the unstated forces at work in the novel. The Tom Buchanans control the legal institutions of this city, while the Meyer Wolfsheims control the underworld.

Led by the Anti-Saloon League, the Eighteenth Amendment to the

Constitution was passed on 16 January 1919 when Nebraska became the thirty-sixth state to ratify it. The Volstead Act, which put legal teeth into the enforcement process, was passed in September 1919. Wilson's veto was overridden by Congress, and the Eighteenth Amendment came into force on 16 January 1920. Prohibition only extended the activities of the New York underworld, which *The Great Gatsby* catches with great precision. The lunch Gatsby and Nick have with Meyer Wolfsheim catches the spirit of Fitzgerald's own meeting with Arnold Rothstein, on whom Wolfsheim is modeled. At the restaurant the killing of Rosey Rosenthal comes up. Herman "Beansy" Rosenthal was a small-time gambler and hood who refused to pay extortion money to one Charles Becker, a lieutenant in the New York police department. Rosenthal threatened to go to the authorities if Becker did not back down, but when threats were made on his life, Rosenthal was the one who backed down. Rothstein advised him to get out of town, even to the point of lending him money, but Rosenthal tried to tough it out. His fatal mistake came when he was persuaded by Herbert Bayard Swope, an editor on the New York *World*, to tell his sensational story to the newspaper, where it appeared in the 13 July 1912 edition. Realizing that he had signed his own death warrant, Rosenthal went to the police and officially gave them the same story. He then walked out onto the streets, went to the Metropole Hotel on West Forty-third Street, ordered a porterhouse steak, and ate his meal as he waited for death to arrive. When told there was someone looking for him outside, Rosenthal walked out of the hotel and into a blizzard of bullets. Four hit men were executed for this murder—and eventually Becker also. Fitzgerald captures the spirit—not the exact facts—of the Rosenthal murder. Three years after the publication of *The Great Gatsby* Arnold Rothstein would also be gunned down for refusing to pay some large gambling debts. Fitzgerald's novel not only caught the sense of the past, it at times caught the sense of the future.

Another event that Fitzgerald's novel seems to catch is the rise of the new movie industry. The movies had begun with the kinetoscope and penny arcade, moved on to the "Electric Theatre" and the "Nickelodeon," and came into their own when director-producers like D. W. Griffith moved away from the fixed camera and used innovative camera techniques, including the close-up, the long shot, the fade-in and fade-out, and high- and low-angle shots. Griffith really was the father of the modern cinema. He discovered Mary Pickford and Lillian Gish, and he made the first twelve-reel movie—the spectacular and controversial *The Birth of a Nation*, based on the Reverend Thomas Dixon's glorification of the Ku Klux Klan in *The Clansman*. Less controversial than Griffith was Allan Dwan, whom Fitzgerald alludes to along with Herbert Bayard Swope in connection with his portrayals of Gatsby's parties. Dwan, who would become a leading director, was just beginning his career at this time. In the course of his long life—he died at the age of ninety-six in December 1981—he directed over four hundred films and oversaw the making of as many more. At the time Fitzgerald knew him, Dwan was directing a movie with Gloria Swanson—and it is most likely that the director and actress that Daisy finds so alluring are Allan Dwan and Gloria Swanson.

The parties themselves were undoubtedly modeled on the lavish affairs hosted by Herbert Bayard Swope, who, as we have seen, was directly involved in the Rosenthal case, a bridge between the underworld and respectable society, and a close friend of Arnold Rothstein. Ring Lardner, Swope's Great Neck neighbor, described Swope parties that would last all weekend with the sky illuminated much like in *The Great Gatsby*. Swope, from a Jewish family in St. Louis, came to New York and became a very successful reporter, winning a Pulitzer Prize for his coverage of international politics before he moved up to executive director of the *World*. Across the bay from his house in Great Neck were the more established estates of the Harrimans, Vanderbilts, Sandfords, Morgans, Guggenheims, Schiffs, and William Randolph Hearst. Fitzgerald did not have to go far to find inspiration for *The Great Gatsby*.

This was an era of radical change—of growth in population, in the gross national product, in the rise of new technology and forms of mass media. In 1920 the population of the United States was 106,466,000; by 1929, 121,770,000. In 1920 the gross national product was $73 billion; in 1929, $104 billion. In 1920 the top five percent controlled 23.96 percent of the wealth; by 1929, 33.49 percent. And as people became richer they paid less taxes under Harding, Coolidge, and Hoover. In

Historical Context

1920 a person making $25,000 paid 11.4 percent of it in taxes; in 1929, 3.4 percent. In 1920 8,131,522 automobiles were registered in the United States; by 1929, 23,120,897—a success story based on the lives of men like William Crapo Durant who formed General Motors in 1908, and Henry Ford who brought out the Model T, the first mass-produced car, in the same year. The new machine brought with it a kind of recklessness, as Fitzgerald's novel would show. In the twenties, on average, 25,000 were killed and 600,000 were injured in automobile accidents each year. The first traffic signals came into being on Broadway in New York: a red light was a warning, green meant go, and white meant stop. This was a vast improvement over the twelve-colored light system at the corner of Tremont and Boylston streets in Boston, which managed only to bewilder the motorist.

Pittsburgh's KDKA became the first licensed radio station in America in October 1920. At the beginning of 1922 there were four licensed stations; by the end of that year there would be 576. Tabloid publishing was a British invention until the New York *Daily News* caught on in 1919. By the mid-twenties New York had three tabloids with a circulation of over 1.6 million. Technology and mass media were beginning to take over America, to shape and determine the collective mind. Critics like H. L. Mencken were most cynical when it came to the matter of mass intelligence. "Nobody ever lost money underestimating the intelligence of the American public," Mencken said—a statement that seems to support the public response to Bruce Barton's *The Man Nobody Knows: A Discovery of the Real Jesus*, a book that argued that Jesus was not really the "lamb of God"—weak, unhappy, glad to die—but a forceful, energetic manager-type, the founder of modern business. Barton's was the best-selling nonfiction book in 1925 (the year *The Great Gatsby* was published) and 1926.

Professional sports was also on the rise in the twenties. Despite the scandal of the fixed World Series of 1919, baseball was more popular than ever. In 1919 the Boston Red Sox traded Babe Ruth to the New York Yankees for $125,000. That year, Ruth hit fifty-four home runs; in 1921 he would hit fifty-nine home runs, and the Yankees would win the pennant for the first time as well as attract 1,289,443 fans to the Polo

Grounds (before Yankee Stadium was built in 1923). Fitzgerald actually set the confrontation scene between Gatsby and Tom Buchanan at a Yankees game and later at a restaurant in Central Park before he changed it in a later draft to the Plaza Hotel. A thematic subcurrent of *The Great Gatsby* involves a sense of a new, urban public manipulated by power brokers, and Nick's sudden awareness that a World Series can be fixed gives him insight into the corruptibility of this vast world. The story of Albert B. Fall, the secretary of the interior who leased government oil reserves for personal "loans" and other favors, only reinforced this sense of corruptibility—and of the fragility of a system that could break like a bubble. That moment came in the autumn of 1929: on 24 October the market was down $5 million, on 28 October it was down another $10 million, and on 29 October stocks collapsed completely. The Jazz Age was over.

The night the stock market crashed, Scott and Zelda Fitzgerald stayed at the Beau Rivage in St. Raphaël, in the room Ring Lardner had previously occupied: "We got out as soon as we could," Fitzgerald would later write in *The Crack-Up*, "because we had been there so many times before—it is sadder to find the past again and find it inadequate to the present than it is to have it elude you and remain forever a harmonious conception of memory."[2] This sense of loss, which Fitzgerald used to describe the end of a decade, the end of an American era, is exactly the same emotion that he delineated so brilliantly in *The Great Gatsby*. The 1920s seen through the prism of Fitzgerald's novel becomes a strange distillation of unlimited wonder and opportunity foundering on human excess and waste, a heightened and yet insubstantial carnivalesque moment in which personal and national desire give way to resplendent emptiness; indeed the twenties may in many ways be thought of as Gatsby's America.

2

The Importance of the Work

Any attempt to pinpoint the importance of a work involves a slightly circular argument. The criteria that one brings to the work establish its sense of importance, and the claim for importance then justifies the criteria. Such a necessary circularity need not, however, diminish the more obvious contexts used in establishing the worth of a literary text. Complexity and artistry, vision and technique are the values usually brought to the evaluative process. But even within these terms critics find room for disagreement. What is narratively complex and artistically accomplished to one may seem simplistic and awkward to another. So at the outset we must be aware that any discussion of the "greatness" of a work involves judgments that are both tentative and personal.

The problem of evaluation is complicated further by the fact that there are many modes of fiction: the early realism of Defoe, for example, functions differently from the comic realism of Dickens, which in turn functions differently from the romantic realism of Hugo, or the naturalism of Zola, or the mythic-symbolism of Joyce. Fitzgerald began his career by writing an aesthetic novel in the tradition of the bildungsroman; moved on to write a seminaturalistic, documentary kind of novel; then under the influence of Conrad, turned to the highly wrought novel of symbolic detail, controlled by the sensibility and moral intelligence of a narrator who participates in the action. Along with the mythic-symbolism of Joyce, the stream of consciousness of Virginia Woolf, the narrative primitivism of D. H. Lawrence, this kind of novel is central to the very idea of the modern, at the same time that it functions differently—and hence must be read and evaluated differently—from the other narrative modes and the subgenres within those modes. *The Great Gatsby* is perhaps the best example of what might be called moral symbolism, and the critics who underestimate this novel tend to do so by not seeing clearly the mode in which it was written—and how successfully that mode was accomplished.

Some of these critics are also put off at the outset by Fitzgerald's reputation, which has been diminished by the short stories—many of them trivial—that he wrote for such popular journals as the *Saturday Evening Post.* Ernest Hemingway always felt superior to him on this score. That Fitzgerald diluted his craft under the urgent pressures of debt and the need for money cannot be denied. That he also wrote a dozen or so of the best short stories in the twentieth century can also not be denied. When he was in control of his craft, Fitzgerald was capable of consistently major achievements.

By 1924 Fitzgerald was in the position to write a masterwork like *Gatsby*—everything had been building toward this moment. He had served a kind of apprenticeship in the writing of his two previous novels, and he had begun to conceptualize the Gatsby novel in such short stories as "Winter Dreams," "The Diamond as Big as the Ritz," "Absolution," and a bit later "The Rich Boy." He would never be so completely in control of his craft again, so sure of the narrative effect that he wanted to create, and in such good health that he would have the energy to work on that novel even at times to the point of exhaustion.

What Fitzgerald did in *The Great Gatsby* was to raise his central character to a mythic level, to reveal a man whose intensity of dream partook of a state of mind that embodied America itself. Gatsby is the last of the romantic heroes, whose energy and sense of commitment take him in search of his personal grail. The quest cannot be separated from the destiny of a nation—from people who came to a new world, crossed a continent, and built a nation. Such an exercise in will was not without consequence, however, for these people left behind a trail of plunder and waste—of Indians massacred, of the land and its minerals exploited, of nature pillaged. Once the frontier was exhausted, the adventurous state of mind still existed; only now the object of its contemplation was less heroic and sometimes even banal. Fitzgerald's Gatsby was a man of such heroic vision without the opportunity to find a commensurate experience for it.

Once the frontier was gone, Gatsby brought his Western intensity East and found a "frontier" equivalent in the New York underworld, the world of professional gamblers, bootleggers, financial schemers, and a new breed of exploiters that the city bred differently from the land. Such a man will stand out in "respectable" company because he will lack social credentials. Novelists like Henry James, E. M. Forster, and Ford Madox Ford gave us insight into how such a highly structured world works; it turns primarily on manners, a system of decorum that those who are within the system share and that separates them from those who are outside. In this world Gatsby is a poseur, a man who fakes it, exploiting his brief contact with Oxford, his war record, and a natural physical elegance that belies his crudity of taste and his lack of a privileged knowledge of manners.

And it is this Gatsby who becomes the object of focus for Nick Carraway—a young, privileged Westerner who has also come East to try his fortune. But Nick does not have to make his own money—that was done by those who came before him, whose crude ventures are now concealed by bourgeois status. Nick's granduncle and father have settled comfortably into the business of American business, of servicing the hardware needs of the new America. Such is a diminished thing. The romantic intensity that the pioneers brought to the new world, Gatsby now brings to a beautiful but also rather superficial, self-involved, self-protecting, morally empty young woman. The power of this novel ultimately comes from the structured relationships between these narrative elements. We have two kinds of seeing in this novel: the visionary whose vision has been emptied, and a moral observer who is initially unsympathetic to what he sees in the visionary ("Gatsby . . . represented everything for which I have an unaffected scorn") but who is eventually won

13

over by what is compelling and poignant in Gatsby's story. Nick comes to see that Gatsby's fate cannot be separated from his own or from the destiny of America—that something heroic has passed in the backwash of time; that in the era of Harding and Coolidge, the era of modern America, a crass materiality has absorbed our attention, making it a dreamer's fate to idealize what is now most hollow in an emptied past. We most often think of the visionary as one who can read the future; but the visionary is really the person who can read the past, who knows what has been used up, what has been materially exhausted and is no longer available. In this context Fitzgerald was truly a visionary.

In *The Great Gatsby* Fitzgerald tells an extremely American story, so much so that he even thought of titling it "Under the Red, White, and Blue." The sense of personal destiny in the novel gives way to a sense of national destiny and that in turn to a romantic state of mind. Fitzgerald's literary imagination was always deeply connected to the romantics; he began reading them seriously at Princeton under the influence of Professor Christian Gauss, and he brought the same intensity of romantic interest to an aesthetic tradition that spawned so many of the young disillusioned men and women that Fitzgerald made the trademark of his fiction. Such disillusionment was imbedded in the vision itself, inseparable from its workings: illusion versus reality, a transcendental ideal in conflict with an earthy materialism, the Keatsian frozen moment in contrast with time the destroyer, the romantic ideal transforming physical reality, the rose elevated beyond the garden—such was the fateful metaphysics behind a novel like *Gatsby*, a metaphysic that gave such tragic priority to the unreal that it was assured the ideal would be undone in time. But to state the problem this bluntly robs it of narrative subtlety, robs it of the greatest gift Fitzgerald brought to his novel—a style so well honed that his story takes on the intensity of a poem.

And indeed it was a poem that served among his models. In *The Great Gatsby* Fitzgerald wrote an American equivalent to *The Waste Land* and brought the same intensity of vision to the postwar, secular world of America that T. S. Eliot had brought to the world of postwar England. So many of the touches in the novel are purely Eliotic—the scene in the Washington Heights apartment where the principals talk about Mrs. Eberhardt, who "goes around looking at people's feet in their own homes" (31), or the counterscene in Daisy's mansion where it is asked, "What'll we do with ourselves this afternoon . . . and the day after that, and the next thirty years?" (118), or the scene involving Nick walking the city streets seeing both from the inside and out. Nick may start off with absolute scorn for Gatsby, but he comes to admire him both as a man and as a portent of America. Nick sees what is both pathetic and grand in the last of the American romantics, the last of the breed with an epic sense of destiny whose vision took him beyond the realm in which the rest of us live. When asked why Daisy married Tom Buchanan, Gatsby responds, "it was only personal." Such touches Fitzgerald brought to every page of *The Great Gatsby*, which radiates with its own special energy.

Fitzgerald's fiction, his conception of character, the narrative unfolding, the complexity of language—all make for a novel of unbelievable complexity. On a personal note, I can say that I have read this novel well over one hundred times, and every time I reread it, I find that I am seeing things that I had previously missed. Few novels—particularly those so seemingly simple on the surface—hold up so well and have the ability to continually surprise us. *The Great Gatsby* seems larger than the criteria that we bring to its evaluation; whatever we say about it seems never complete or satisfactory enough. It is a novel that has continually proved itself larger than its many critics, which is perhaps what we mean when we speak of it as a masterpiece. When the canon of American literature changes, the criteria we use to establish that canon change as well. Literary posterity is always a fragile thing, but challenges to the permanence of *The Great Gatsby* seem to cast more doubt on our critical criteria than they do on Fitzgerald's achievement.

3

Critical Reception

It is hard for a reader today to realize that when F. Scott Fitzgerald died in December 1940, all of his books were out of print, including the fourth printing of *The Great Gatsby*, the 1934 Modern Library edition, which Random House had let go out of print because it was not selling well. Today *The Great Gatsby* sells over three hundred thousand copies a year, and over three hundred critical essays have been written about it since Fitzgerald's death. It took a long time for the greatness of *Gatsby* to emerge, but that question is no longer in doubt. One might, however, have resisted giving it such permanent status after reading the initial reviews. The reviewer for the Raleigh *News and Observer*, for example, complained that everybody in this novel is "more or less rotten" (3 May 1925); the reviewer for the Kansas City *Star* declared that the novel was "so sordid and depressing that if the cleverness is there it is obscured by the details of [the] story" (9 May 1925); the headlines of the New York *World* announced "F. Scott Fitzgerald's Latest Dud" (12 April 1925); the Boston *Evening Transcript* predicted that *Gatsby* "will not be counted among those novels which make up a small list of the distinguished fiction of the season" (23 May 1925); the Milwaukee *Journal* dismissed it as too "contemporary. . . . It is only as permanent as a newspaper story, and as on the surface" (1 May 1925). One can laugh in retrospect at such assessments, except that many of these judgments were shared by the more prestigious critics of the era. H. L. Mencken, whom Fitzgerald much admired at this time, declared *Gatsby* no more than "a glorified anecdote," made up of characters (with the exception of Gatsby) who are "mere marionettes." The story, Mencken continued, "does not go below the surface" (Baltimore *Evening Sun*, 2 May 1925). While Mencken praised the "gusto" of the novel, its "sharp accuracy," and its "fine texture," he clearly thought it was trivial—and his judgment was generally shared by reviewers. There were, however, a number of dissenters, including William Rose Benet who saw the maturity of the novel and praised its "pace . . . and . . . admirable control" (*Saturday Review of Literature*, 9 May 1925), and Gilbert Seldes, who in retrospect seems prophetic when he wrote, "*The Great Gatsby* is a brilliant work, and it is also a sound one; it is carefully written, and vivid; it has structure, and it has life. To all the talents, discipline has been added" (*New Criterion*, January 1926). But such enthusiasm was decidedly in the minority.

Questions emerge: why did the greatness of *The Great Gatsby* take so long to become established, and what was it that led to our present understanding and appreciation of the novel? A reevaluation did not take place until about ten years after Fitzgerald's death, at which time there was a renewed interest in the man. This interest came about in part through Edmund Wilson's editing of *The Crack-Up* in 1945, the popularity of Budd Schulberg's novel *The Disenchanted* (1950), which dealt in semifictional terms with a drunken episode Fitzgerald experienced while on a Hollywood assignment, and the publication of Arthur Mizener's biography *The Far Side of Paradise* (1951). The sudden interest in the man brought a renewed interest in the work, and it is not surprising that the first critical essays connected the tragic sense of Fitzgerald's life to his novels and stories. Representative was an essay like William Troy's "Scott Fitzgerald—the Authority of Failure" (*Accent*, Autumn 1945). Lionel Trilling barely shifted ground when he found a "heroic quality" in *The Crack-Up* essays, which he connected to a tradition of romantic tragedy (*Nation*, 25 August 1945) and which he later applied to a reading of *Gatsby* (Introduction, New Directions edition, 1945). Trilling later reworked this material into an extended essay that he published in *The Liberal Imagination*—an essay that so offended Edward Dahlberg that he wrote his own dissent, attacking Fitzgerald's "peopleless fiction," insisting that *The Great Gatsby* is "a novel without ideas," and calling Trilling "Mr. Sieve-Mind" for his praise of Fitzgerald (*The Freeman*, 5 November 1951).

Feelings about Fitzgerald the man and his work obviously ran high, and the discussion would probably have continued on the biographical plane except for the rise of the New Criticism with its emphasis on the formal nature of the work—an emphasis for which *The Great Gatsby* was made to order. The closer the scrutiny, the better the novel held up, and *The Great Gatsby* was reborn under the critical examination of such essays as Marius Bewley's "Scott Fitzgerald's Criticism of America" (*Sewanee Review*, 1954), Edwin Fussell's "Fitzgerald's Brave New World" (*English Literary History*, 1952), and Robert Stallman's "Gatsby and the Hole in Time" (*Modern Fiction Studies*, 1955). While all of these studies were concerned with the form and texture of the novel, Bewley and Fussell treated its social content, and Stallman treated the theme of romantic time. After this kind of careful critical attention, Fitzgerald's readers brought a more intense understanding to the text, and no longer could *Gatsby* be dismissed as a novel of trivial "anecdote," all surface and no substance.

These critical essays were substantiated by full-length critical studies. James E. Miller's *The Fictional Technique of Scott Fitzgerald* (1957, revised edition 1964) traced the literary influence of H. G. Wells, H. L. Mencken, Joseph Conrad, Willa Cather, Edith Wharton, and Henry James on the novels up to *Gatsby* (supplemented in the later edition by essays on *Tender Is the Night* and *The Last Tycoon*). Kenneth Eble's *F. Scott Fitzgerald* (1963) analyzed the work primarily in the context of Fitzgerald's life, although his discussion of *Gatsby* in *American Literature* (1964) was one of the first genetic readings of the novel. Henry Dan Piper's *F. Scott Fitzgerald: A Critical Portrait* (1965) continued the tendency to combine biography with critical exegesis; and Sergio Perosa's *The Art of F. Scott Fitzgerald* (also 1965) discussed the interconnectedness of the writing. My own *F. Scott Fitzgerald and the Craft of Fiction*

(1966) also moved from the man to the work, suggesting the emotional origins of the themes that dominated the Fitzgerald canon. Robert Sklar's *F. Scott Fitzgerald: The Last Laocoon* (1967) brought the Fitzgerald papers at Princeton more into play and—despite the dubious claim that Fitzgerald's fiction is a systematic reworking of the genteel hero—gave us a sense of the cultural materials that informed the fiction. Milton Hindus's *F. Scott Fitzgerald: An Introduction and Interpretation* (1968) relied heavily on a discussion of plot and biographical information in its attempt to locate Fitzgerald in the "backwash" of the romantic movement.

At this point, the criticism moved toward a cultural and historical context. Milton Stern's *The Golden Moment: The Novels of F. Scott Fitzgerald* (1970) discussed Fitzgerald the man in the context of his fiction and connected matters biographical, fictional, and historical, seeing in the fiction an identity crisis that was peculiarly American and thus inseparable from the "uses of history, the American identity, and the moral reconstruction of the American past." The emphasis upon the historical context was carried even further by John Callahan's *The Illusion of a Nation: Myth and History in the Novels of F. Scott Fitzgerald* (1972), a reading that was certainly correct in connecting Fitzgerald's novels with themes in history, but a reading that has not worn well, perhaps because it connected Fitzgerald's fiction too facilely with the events of the 1960s. Joan Allen's *Candles and Carnival Lights: The Catholic Sensibility of F. Scott Fitzgerald* (1978) swung us back toward biography by treating the fiction in the context of Fitzgerald's Catholic upbringing. Robert Emmet Long's *The Achieving of "The Great Gatsby," 1920–1925* (1979) picked up where James E. Miller and Kenneth Eble left off, giving us a study of the apprentice years, the influence of Conrad, and a discussion of what changes in the *Gatsby* manuscript tell us about Fitzgerald's fictional method. Brian Way's *F. Scott Fitzgerald and the Art of Social Fiction* (1980) moved us away from both biographical and influence studies to a study of Fitzgerald as a social novelist in the tradition of Henry James, Henry Adams, and Edith Wharton.

While these studies concentrated primarily on the fiction, the interest in biography tended to dominate the discussion, and the most extended work on Fitzgerald was biographical. While one or two of these works are models of biographical methodology, the same picture tended to emerge. Perhaps the first portrait, by Mizener, was too strong to dislodge. Mizener gave us a portrait of a man who was unable to minister his talents and wasted them away. This portrait is intensified by Sheilah Graham and Gerold Frank in *Beloved Infidel* (1958), which gives a personal account of Miss Graham's stormy relationship with Fitzgerald during his Hollywood years. Andrew Turnbull's *Scott Fitzgerald* (1962) also relied on personal experience to inform his discussion, especially his friendship with Fitzgerald during the thirties, when Fitzgerald was renting a house on the Turnbull estate. And Sara Mayfield's *Exiles from Paradise: Zelda and Scott Fitzgerald* (1971) again makes use of her personal friendship with Zelda to give a stark portrait of a bitter and destructive marriage, a portrait that is etched again in Nancy Milford's *Zelda: A Biography* (1970), and even once again in James R. Mellow's *Invented Lives* (1984). Scott Donaldson's *Fool for Love* (1983) once again treated Fitzgerald's relationship with women, but also gave us useful insight into his Princeton days. Andre Le Vot's *F. Scott Fitzgerald: A Biography* (1979, translated 1983) was good on the European years, especially such matters as Zelda's affair with Edouard Jozan, an incident in Fitzgerald's life that came simultaneously with his writing about adultery in *The Great Gatsby*. But the most impressive of the recent biographies of Fitzgerald is Matthew J. Bruccoli's *Some Sort of Epic Grandeur: The Life of F. Scott Fitzgerald* (1981), an extremely detailed and informed account of Fitzgerald's life, which, besides giving us the best discussion that we have of the bibliographical history of Fitzgerald's writing, reminds us that despite the travail, the drunkenness, the sickness, the wasted genius, a kind of epic courage allowed Fitzgerald to complete work and to go on in ways that would have defeated a less courageous man. Bruccoli's is an honest portrait and does not spare us the now too well known details of dissipation and moments of meanness.

Indeed, the image of the man that emerges from almost all of these biographies is not a pleasant one. From his mid-twenties on, Fitzgerald's life was controlled by liquor. Once drunk, he was often a mean drunk, and the biographical accounts are punctuated by a kind of ritualistic letter that Fitzgerald would write the morning after in which he would apologize to guests and hosts alike after a night of unpleasant behavior. One cannot truly calculate the wasted energy that went into such activity, energy never brought to his serious work. And such waste seemed to find a parallel in wasted money. Fitzgerald once complained that he could not live on $36,000 a year, despite the fact that such a sum was then worth about ten times its current spending value. If Fitzgerald had nurtured his income, had avoided the sustained drunks, he would have written far more serious fiction than we have—and would probably have dominated in reputation his literary contemporaries. But to bewail this loss is, ironically, to evoke a constant theme of the fiction, for there is no question that Fitzgerald wrote directly out of his own sense of experience. All of this leads to a cruel dilemma: the man who came to understand the tragedy of waste had to waste his creative genius to come by such an understanding. Perhaps this kind of dilemma is inseparable from the artistic process, which feeds on what is destructive in the artist himself. Certainly this seems to be so with Fitzgerald; the insight into the cruel process of waste that so informs his fiction was an insight paid for at the highest price.

Perhaps only the compilers and bibliographers have labored more strenuously than Fitzgerald's biographers, and here once again Matthew J. Bruccoli has led the way. His work in clearing the underbrush goes far beyond the capacity that we usually assign to one man. In 1972 he gave us a descriptive bibliography, which was supplemented in 1980; in 1972 he edited the letters between Fitzgerald and his agent Harold Ober; in 1973 he edited Fitzgerald's Ledger (a kind of diary) and in 1978 Fitzgerald's Notebooks; in 1979 he collected the last of the uncollected stories in *The Price Was High*; and in 1980 he edited, with Margaret M. Duggan, the correspondence, expanding the record far beyond the Turnbull edition of 1963. His work on *The Great Gatsby* has been equally energetic: in 1973 gave us a facsimile edition of the holograph and in 1974 the *Apparatus for F. Scott Fitzgerald's "The Great Gatsby" [Under the Red, White, and Blue]*, which involved an Introduction that discussed the novel's composition, an apparatus of textual notes, and a list of emendations that will allow the reader enough knowledge of the 1925 first-printed edition to make corrections in the Scribner Library edition. Jackson R. Bryer has also labored hard in giving us useful bibliographical information. His *Critical Reputation of F. Scott Fitzgerald: A Bibliographical Study* (1967), with a supplement through 1981 (1984), gives us a summary of the major criticism, and his *F. Scott Fitzgerald: The Critical Reception* (1978) collects the major reviews of Fitzgerald's books. Along with Bruccoli, Bryer has edited *F. Scott Fitzgerald in His Own Time: A Miscellany* (1971), which gives us previously uncollected writings by Fitzgerald, including his journalistic pieces, interviews, and published commentary. Bryer has also edited *The Short Stories of F. Scott Fitzgerald: New Approaches in Criticism* (1982), which comes with an exhaustive checklist of all the criticism on the stories. Other important editorial work involves John Kuehl's *The Apprentice Fiction of F. Scott Fitzgerald 1909–1917* (1965), which reprints the early stories and discusses how they anticipate the later work, including *The Great Gatsby*. A. Scott Berg's *Maxwell Perkins: Editor of Genius* (1978) gives us an informed study of the relationship between Fitzgerald and his influential editor, whose presence had a tremendous effect on *The Great Gatsby*. And Andrew T. Crossland has produced a concordance to *The Great Gatsby* (1975).

Biographically, critically, and bibliographically, Fitzgerald has been well served by his scholars and critics. If the fascination with the man has been a bit obsessive, it has led to a critical context that has often informed the fiction. But as useful as the biography may be, we have reached the point where we must accept the fact that novels like *The Great Gatsby* have a life of their own, independent of the man who created them. We have had few studies of Fitzgerald in relation to the history of the novel or the history of Western culture. This may be the next direction that Fitzgerald criticism takes, for Fitzgerald constantly saw himself and his work as inseparable from American history and saw American history as inseparable from Western culture. We tend to forget that he spent almost all of the twenties in Europe, and this experience not only acquainted him with a different culture and history but intensified his feelings about his own history and culture. Near the end of his life he tellingly summarized this idea in his notebook:

Critical Reception

I look out at it [American history]—and I think it is the most beautiful history in the world. It is the history of me and my people. And if I came here yesterday . . . I should still think so. It is the history of all aspiration—not just the American dream but the human dream and if I came at the end of it that too is a place in the line of pioneers.[3]

A READING

F. Scott Fitzgerald arriving in Europe in the mid-1920s with wife, Zelda, and daughter, "Scottie."

4

The Road to West Egg

He had come a long way to this blue lawn, and his dream must have seemed so close that he could hardly fail to grasp it. He did not know that it was already behind him. . . . (182)

F. Scott Fitzgerald came upon the idea for *The Great Gatsby* in the summer of 1922, while he was living at White Bear Lake in Minnesota. At that time he wrote Maxwell Perkins, his editor at Scribner's, that he had plans for a novel: "Its locale will be the middle west and New York at 1885. It will concern less superlative beauties than I run to usually and will be centered on a smaller period of time. It will have a catholic element."[4] Fitzgerald's description is hardly an accurate reflection of the novel that he would complete over two years later, and yet a number of key themes in *The Great Gatsby* can be traced to this comment. Embedded in his original idea is a novel involving a contrast between East and West, suggesting themes relevant to the Gilded Age. That summer he would write "Winter Dreams," the story that most directly anticipates *Gatsby*, so the theme of romantic betrayal seems also to have been part of his early conception of the novel. In October 1922 the Fitzgeralds moved to Great Neck, on Long Island, forty-five minutes by car from New York City, a suburb made elegant by a good deal of "new" money that came with the postwar boom in the movies, journalism, and advertising. Once back in New York, the "Catholic" element in the novel seems to have become more remote, although a religious theme is certainly an important subcurrent in *The Great Gatsby*. At this time Fitzgerald excised a long section of the novel dealing with Gatsby's Catholic boyhood, which he published independently in H.L. Mencken's *American Mercury*. Before he could get deeply into his new novel, he was distracted by his play, *The Vegetable*. He had great financial hopes invested in this play, and when it failed in Atlantic City in November 1923, he was both professionally and financially disappointed. He spent the next five months writing stories to get out of debt, and it was not until April 1924 that he returned in earnest to his novel. At that time he wrote Perkins, "I feel I have an enormous power in me now." He goes on to say, "in my new novel I'm thrown directly on purely creative work—not trashy imaginings as in my stories but the sustained imagination of a sincere and radiant world."[5]

In many ways Fitzgerald was moving into new narrative terrain, since his new novel would be a radical departure from *This Side of Paradise* (1920) and *The Beautiful and Damned* (1922). The former novel was almost a pure bildungsroman in the tradition of Compton MacKenzie, whom Fitzgerald unashamedly imitated, and the latter concerned physical and emotional deterioration in the manner of Dreiser and Norris, whose work was celebrated by H. L. Mencken, whom Fitzgerald much admired at this time. But his new novel was to be consciously different. "I want to write something *new*," Fitzgerald wrote Perkins in July 1922, "something extraordinary and beautiful and simple and intricately patterned."[6]

The tradition of the novel with which Fitzgerald seems to be working here was that of Joseph Conrad, as Conrad had defined it in his preface to *The Nigger of the Narcissus*, an essay Fitzgerald refers to constantly, especially Conrad's belief that the artist "speaks to our capacity for delight and wonder, to the sense of mystery surrounding our lives; to our sense of pity, and beauty, and pain . . . and to the subtle but invincible conviction of solidarity that knits together the loneliness of innumerable hearts, to the solidarity in dreams, in joy, in sorrow, in aspirations, in illusions, in hope, in fear which binds men to each other, which binds together all humanity—the dead to the living and the living to the unborn."[7]

In order to convey this sense of mystery, wonder, aspiration, and the solidarity of human nature, Fitzgerald believed that he would need a new technique, one that Conrad himself had used but that Fitzgerald felt must be adapted to his own purposes. Such a technique would involve creating a character, like Kurtz or Lord Jim, who was slightly larger than life (what critics would later call "mythic" in nature), who lived or felt with an intensity that separated him from others, who did not fully understand the complexity of his own being, and who would be seen by a narrator who was trying to make sense out of such monomania and to draw a moral lesson from it that might have application, on a lower frequency, to his own sense of life.

Such a story would be essentially tragic, by which Fitzgerald meant that such a character would undo himself, and such a novel would end on a "dying fall," by which he in turn meant that a sense of sadness and melancholy came about when such intensity was deflected by the opposing forces of life. This new kind of novel would work in great part by association and suggestion; the major character would be more mysterious than fully blown and the reader would be expected to fill in the narrative gaps that the author intentionally left in the text. But Fitzgerald also believed that he had to know the material that he was leaving out as well as the material that he was developing, that the empty spaces of a text spoke as loudly as those that were filled, so long as an author had clearly in mind the narrative meaning he was consciously omitting.

With this general plan in mind Fitzgerald began to formulate the narrative design of *The Great Gatsby*. Gatsby would, of course, be in the center of the novel. Gatsby would in effect be the product of his own imagination, a creature who wanted to live with the greatest intensity of romantic experience. In his early fiction Fitzgerald had conceptualized an idea of self based on the principles of "personage" versus "personality." By *personage* he meant a sense of an essential self that made one different from others and gave total focus to one's purpose and sense of meaning in life. By *personality* he meant a sense of an accidental self that was composed of the by-products of personage: the manner in which one spoke, the way one carried oneself while walking or dancing, the way one dressed. Fitzgerald felt that only the personage lived life with intensity.

The personage became his own god, had a sense of the vast potentiality of life.

When one lost that sense of life or promise—which Fitzgerald characteristically predicated on youth—then life lost its sense of wonder, its splendor, its romantic promise. To desire was, ironically, more important than to have. The man who had great wealth (Tom Buchanan) or the man who was beaten by life (George Wilson) lacked the intensity of experience of a Gatsby who was a "son of God" and who "sprang from his Platonic conception of himself," as the novel tells us. To lose this romantic conception of self is to move from a kind of heaven of the mind to a hell, which in the novel is embodied by the valley of ashes and incarnated by George Wilson its custodian, who, appropriately, becomes the agent of Gatsby's death when Gatsby himself loses his sense of wonder and romantic readiness, at which moment Gatsby's world becomes "material without being real" and a rose becomes "grotesque."

No modern novelist has conveyed the meaning of the romantic imagination better than Fitzgerald, whose interest in Keats, Pater, Wilde, and Dowson has long been documented. It is exactly this sense of romantic possibility that leads Gatsby to invent himself at the age of seventeen. In order to invent himself, he has to repudiate his physical father, as the final chapter of the novel so poignantly suggests, and to create a series of new fathers. The first of the new fathers is Dan Cody, whose name (Daniel Boone "Buffalo Bill" Cody) suggests the beginning and end of the frontier. Fitzgerald, it seems clear, was well aware of Frederick Jackson Turner's thesis that the frontier in America had closed in 1893. No longer could Gatsby go, like Cody, to the frontier to realize himself and forge his destiny. Instead he had to turn to the city, which had eclipsed the frontier, and there enter the world of Tom Buchanan and Meyer Wolfsheim. It is Wolfsheim who becomes a kind of second father ("'I raised him out of nothing'"), the same Wolfsheim who is a lord of the underworld, a denizen of Forty-second Street and the world of Broadway, a world that West Egg comes to embody with its inhabitants of not just new but (in the case of Gatsby) illegal wealth.

The Great Gatsby is a novel without a moral center, and to that extent is very different from the narrative traditions of comic realism and the novel of manners. In the novels of Henry Fielding or Jane Austen there is a Squire Allworthy or a Mr. Knightley who embodies the values to which the plot eventually returns. In the novels of Dickens a sense of sentiment—a rightness of the heart—seems to direct the actions of Esther Summerson or Joe Gargery. In Henry James the social sense is more complex and ambiguous, but Christopher Newman, Isabel Archer, and Lambert Strether have a residual sense of right and wrong which they claim or to which they remain true. In creating himself, Gatsby had no social or moral context to give his intensity direction. He lacked the world of the estate that informed the novels of Fielding and Austen, lacked the faculty of sentiment that led Dickens's characters to resist in-stinctively the evil encountered, lacked the residual values of an aristo-cratic or Puritan heritage that so complexly informed James's characters. Even as a product of romantic vision, Gatsby lacked the aesthetic values of a Pater or a Wilde, because he lacked the education that would differ-entiate genuine from ersatz beauty and, hence, he went about in "service of a vast, vulgar, and meretricious beauty" (99). Gatsby had no residual values to give his life direction except the values he created in inventing himself—and these were marred by the serious conflict between his es-sential self (personage) and accidental self (personality) and by a world devoid of the romantic sense of good, the beauty and truth that incar-nated and hence justified the intensity of his vision. It is Daisy Fay who becomes the incarnation of his romantic ideal: Daisy, five years married to Tom Buchanan; Daisy, who will at last resort protect herself no matter who or what she has to abandon; Daisy, who lacks maturity, intrinsic worth, or solidity of character. And why should she be better than the world of which she is a part? It is Gatsby who endows her with a meaning that she could in no way embody. "I wouldn't ask too much of her," Nick Carraway warns the unheeding Gatsby (111).

While *The Great Gatsby* lacks a moral center, the novel—in the tra-dition of Conrad's Marlow stories—tries to supply such a context for the reader in the person of Nick Carraway. Nick's storytelling occurs after Gatsby is dead, and he begins on a note of moral urgency. He wants the world in "uniform and at a sort of moral attention forever" (2). He is not quite sure himself what is to be the basis for conduct "founded on the hard rock" of moral principle, except perhaps some vague sense of aristocratic behavior left over from the Dukes of Buccleuch, from whom he may have descended, before such aristocracy played itself out in the wholesale hardware business after, significantly, the Civil War, which marked the end in America of the old aristocratic way of life. Fitzgerald had thought his own father had a residue of such values, the "old courtesies," as he called them, connected with the Scott Keys and the Southern aristocracy that he traced through his ancestors. But Fitzgerald well knew that such values had been left in the backwash of time and were arrived at nostalgically by beating on, "boats against the current," born back into a lost past. How much Nick is able to bring a moral sense into play becomes one of the key issues—and narrative problems—of the novel. He claims to be "one of the few honest people that I have ever known" (60), a claim that Jordan Baker disputes at the end of the novel (179), and a claim—the justification or lack of which—that has divided readers since the publication of the novel.

The issue of what to make of Nick as both character and moral reflector is an important one because it is through his eyes that we see the narrative action. And it is not insignificant that Nick tells us throughout that his vision is sometimes blurred and distorted. In a world without a moral center such distortions are perhaps inevitable. At one point Tom Buchanan and Myrtle Wilson commit adultery while Nick sits outside their bedroom reading *Simon Called Peter*, a popular religious novel about an English clergyman who becomes disillusioned and loses his faith once he has experienced the absurdity of war. Published in September 1921, it had gone into its seventy-seventh printing by March 1923, a remarkable figure given the confusion (as Nick indicates) in the way the novel unfolds. Fitzgerald was here clearly satirizing the treacle that passed for a religious experience in the mind of the populace. *The Great Gatsby* was one of the very first novels to depict the vacuousness of the new commercial culture. Except for Gatsby's godlike sense of the potentiality of self, God has withdrawn from this world and is replaced by the commercial billboard with the blind eyes of T. J. Eckleburg, and embodied (all symbolic forms in the novel have human equivalents) by the equally blind eyes of the owl-eyed man who appears at Gatsby's party and reappears at his funeral, bridging the connection between the two, just as the end product of Gatsby's parties are embodied in the orange pulps and lemon rinds and by that other symbol of romantic waste and emotional exhaustion—the valley of ashes. This is a blind world because there is no source of moral vision. This is a wasteland world of exhausted hopes because the only vision to be had—Gatsby's—is an ersatz one. Fitzgerald had encountered these themes before—in T. S. Eliot's *The Waste Land*—but he gave them narrative intensity and their own embodiment in *The Great Gatsby,* which is certainly why Eliot responded so enthusiastically to this novel, calling it the first major step in American fiction since Henry James.

As with Eliot's Tiresias, this is a world of the blind without the redeeming quality of moral vision. It is a novel where crucial scenes turn—as in the scene with the death of Myrtle Wilson—on seeing and misseeing and where this kind of physical opacity has its moral counterpart. The moral carelessness of the novel is in great part carried by the motif of careless driving, suggesting the rise of power (here embodied in the machine) without a sense of responsibility or of human welfare. Jordan Baker (named after two automobiles) becomes the embodiment of such carelessness until that role is taken over by Daisy, who runs over Myrtle in the machine, and by Tom, who allows another man to die for a crime he never committed. "They were careless people" (180), Nick tells us at the novel's close, in a passage that summarizes a sense of power run amok, of selfishness that preempts all other matters, and of complete moral abandonment.

The Great Gatsby is thus a novel about intense romantic commitment without the physical and moral embodiment for such commitment. It is a novel about the romantic intensity of self divorced from an object commensurate to that vision. It is thus a novel about self without object, of ideal separated from reality, vision inseparable from illusion. Ideals are located in an exhausted past that gives the future all the palpability of a mirage. In writing *The Great Gatsby* Fitzgerald gave birth to the nowhere hero, located between a dead past and an implausible future.

In *The Great Gatsby* Fitzgerald was working with many important subtexts, perhaps most important the fate of enlightenment optimism and enlightenment man. With the breakdown of the feudal world, birth rights gave way to "natural" rights, which is only another way of saying that a new kind of man was now free to invent himself. Nearly simultaneously with this radical change in the idea of self, the American continent invited the adventurous to fulfill that sense of self in a new world. This remarkable age of freedom spawned a new nation based on a heightened sense of self and an open frontier. When this frontier was closed, a dimension of self—as well as of place—was shut off. A major cultural change occurred as the source of wealth moved from the land (West) to the city (East). The function of such a city was primarily to process wealth, and such a city gave rise to social institutions, class hierarchies, and a sense of stratification that never existed on the frontier. A young man like Gatsby came now to the city, not the frontier, to fulfill his heightened sense of self—came not to the world of Dan Cody and James J. Hill but to that of Meyer Wolfsheim and Tom Buchanan. Gatsby never understood this important cultural change, but Fitzgerald did. He saw that in the death of Gatsby not only a certain kind of romantic individual was passing but also a whole way of life and state of mind. An object of attainment commensurate with Gatsby's romantic sense of promise had been lost in the backrush of time, just as the romantic sense of wonder of the first sailors to see the American shore was lost with the final settling of America—the closing of the frontier and the end of the Jeffersonian vision, the rise of the new city, and the triumph of the Hamiltonian view. *The Great Gatsby* is thus much more than a novel about the last of the romantics. It is also a novel about America and the state of mind, concept of self, and the realm of possibility that made America possible—made America, for a moment in time, unique in world history. Nick Carraway realizes that the passing of Gatsby is sad, but he further realizes that the passing of what Gatsby stood for is even sadder.

5

A Son of God

The truth was that Jay Gatsby of West Egg, Long Island, sprang from
his Platonic conception of himself. He was a son of God. . . . (99)

In one of the biographical recollections that Nick Carraway gives, he
tells us that Gatsby "was a son of God" and that "he must be about His
Father's business." The Father's business turns out to be the pursuit of a
"vast, vulgar, and meretricious beauty" (99). Gatsby's resolve comes at
the moment he invents himself—"so he invented just the sort of Jay
Gatsby that a seventeen-year-old boy would be likely to invent"—and
this moment comes simultaneously with Gatsby's meeting Dan Cody.
Once this equation is in place, Dan Cody takes on godlike proportions,
and his business—the exploitation of America—becomes Gatsby's business as well, even to the extent that Gatsby creates the kind of self necessary for such a pursuit.

In making this connection so skillfully in *Gatsby*, Fitzgerald links
mythic and historical themes, creating a sense of destiny that is inseparable from the idea of godhead, nation, and self. That these ideas were
deep in Fitzgerald's imagination when he was writing *The Great Gatsby*
can be seen by what underlay the short stories that were written contem-
poraneously with his novel. "Absolution" is most to the point here.
Ultimately published as a short story, it was originally written as a part of
the novel that explored Gatsby's boyhood. Fitzgerald decided to delete

the segment from the novel and to publish it in the June 1924 issue of Mencken's the *American Mercury*. The Gatsby figure—renamed Rudolph Miller—in this story has deliberately lied in the confessional and then received holy communion the next day. Rudolph is the son of Carl Miller, an immigrant to the Midwest, a freight agent with a burnt-out sense of hope. The father is energized, but just barely, by two objects of belief—his faith in the Roman Catholic Church and his "mystical worship of the Empire Builder, James J. Hill," who embodied all that Miller was not.[8] Rudolph is so embarrassed by his father that he has trouble believing that he is his son. In order to give vitality to his own life, Rudolph has invented a second self, which he has named Blatchford Sarnemington, whose heightened sense of possibilities allows "a suave nobility" to flow through him.

It is this heightened imagination that has, in part, led to the inventions in the confessional and the source of guilt that nags Rudolph. When he confesses this state of mind to Father Adolphous Schwartz, the priest tells him not to be so literal-minded, that life is best lived on the level of imagination, and that he need not fret about his deceptions: "It's a thing like a fair, only much more glittering" (*Stories*, 171). The priest tells Rudolph to go to the fair and to see it at a distance, see it "just hang out there in the night like a colored balloon—like a big yellow lantern on a pole." Do not "get up close . . . because if you do you'll only feel the heat and the sweat and the life" (*Stories*, 171). Although the priest is on the verge of a nervous breakdown, what he tells Rudolph (and by extension Gatsby) is that "there was something ineffably gorgeous" (a word Nick uses to describe Gatsby) "somewhere that had nothing to do with God" (*Stories*, 171). It is not the idea of God that energizes the living but the idea of Christ—God made incarnate. Rudolph's father is moved by God and James J. Hill and remains "ineffectual" (*Stories*, 166), while Gatsby turns himself into a son of God, becomes a kind of James J. Hill–Dan Cody figure, and is energized to the point that "his dream must have seemed so close that he could hardly fail to grasp it" (182).

Religious imagery abounds in Fitzgerald's work, as "The Diamond as Big as the Ritz," another of *The Great Gatsby* satellite stories, suggests. In order to get to Braddock Washington's diamond mountain, one has to pass through a valley village, named Fish (which lay under "a poisoned sky . . . minute, dismal, and forgotten").[9] Like the valley of ashes in *The Great Gatsby*, Fish sits beside the railroad tracks, and twelve men gather "like ghosts" at the shanty depot to watch the passing of the seven o'clock train from Chicago. On occasion, "the Great Brakeman" stops at their village to let off a stray passenger, to the bemusement of the twelve villagers. These modern apostles have lost their Christ. Exhausted by life, they have no illusion to give life meaning or interest. As Fitzgerald put it, "there remained in them none of the vital quality of illusion which would make them wonder or speculate, else a religion might have grown up around these mysterious visitations. But the men of Fish were beyond all religion—the barest and most savage tenets of even Christianity could gain no foothold on that barren rock—so there was no altar, no priest, no sacrifice; only each night at seven the silent concourse by the shanty depot, a congregation who lifted up a prayer of dim, anaemic wonder" (*Stories*, 8). Mr. Washington's diamond mountain—symbol of an all-powerful, undeniable materiality—has drained the village of sustenance, emptied it of meaning, and robbed God of embodiment.

In *The Great Gatsby* the function of the exhausted apostles is taken over by George Wilson, who also sits in front of his garage—between the railroad tracks and the road—watching the traffic go by. He is described as "one of these worn-out men" who "sat on a chair in the doorway and stared at the people and the cars that passed along the road" (137). His position is to minister to the machine—not the transcontinental express as in "Diamond"—but the new automobile traffic. The valley town of Fish has given way to the valley of ashes through which one has to go to make the circuitous journey from Gatsby's or Tom Buchanan's house to New York and back. Wilson and his wife live in "a small block of yellow brick," one section of which is their garage, another an all-night restaurant, and the third empty and for rent. Surrounded by a "waste land" and "contiguous to absolutely nothing," Wilson's world ministers to "Main Street," a reference that locates him among the middle class. Rudolph's father (whom George Wilson closely resembles physically), the twelve men of Fish, and Wilson all have been exhausted by those to whom they minister—the Braddock Washingtons, the James J. Hills, and the Tom

Buchanans. Indeed, not only have they been robbed of God, they have failed also to find a sense of wonder that they can incarnate—failed, that is, to find a romantic substitute for God, as the priest advises Rudolph. As a result, the world has become the equivalent of hell, suggested by "the ash-gray men [who] swarm up with leaden spades [like devils] and stir up an impenetrable cloud" of dust (23). In "The Diamond as Big as the Ritz" John T. Unger (Jaunty Hunger) was also from Hades because his family lacked the wealth, and hence the credentials, that would take him beyond his middle-class origins.

Fitzgerald's religious imagery here seems to share much with the ideas Henry Adams set forth in his "Virgin and the Dynamo" chapter in *The Autobiography*. The idea of the Virgin not only gave coherence to the Middle Ages, it energized a historical moment by giving rise to the mythic imagination. Adams was not celebrating the Catholic idea of the Virgin (he actually was reading books on the queen bee when writing that chapter); he was celebrating instead what the imagination can give consent to in order to create a sense of cultural unity, in order to drive an age with a sense of cultural purpose. Columbus, the Crusaders, Charlemagne—all marched or sailed under the banner of the Virgin Mary. Such mythic unity was displaced by the dynamo or the machine. Instead of energizing the imagination, the dynamo feeds off of natural resources, depletes the physical world, creates the valley of ashes and wastelands of modern literature, and allows a sense of unity to give way to multiplicity and indirection. Modern man not only loses God, but he loses the means of finding a substitute for God, by which Fitzgerald meant the means of incarnating his life with a sense of wonder.

It is in this sense that Gatsby is a "son of God." That the object of his desires is not commensurate with this sense of wonder is both sad and a commentary on the age of the dynamo (that is, the modern age) itself. But what is sadder is the state of mind of Carl Miller, the men from Fish, or George Wilson, men who in losing God incarnate have lost a sense of pure possibility. Life has become as gray and somber for them as the gray dust that creates the "impenetrable cloud" in the valley of ashes and obscures the horizon. These men have been exhausted not only of ambition but also of a sense of wonder, of life's promises and hopes. They have lost the sense of possibility and have become as functionary as the machines to which they minister.

This loss of mythic/religious vision in the novel is embodied by the billboard eyes of Dr. T. J. Eckleburg, blue and gigantic, their retinas one yard high, put there by a Queens oculist who perhaps "then sank down himself into eternal blindness" his eyes remaining to "brood" over a "dumping ground" (23). When in chapter 7 Gatsby and Daisy leave New York on the fateful drive that takes Myrtle's life, it is seven o'clock— exactly the time the men of Fish gather to watch the train pass—a time when the light of day is appropriately fading into dusk, seemingly a perpetual condition in the valley of ashes. It is into this "dusk" (138) that Myrtle Wilson rushes, hoping to be saved from her hell, only to be crushed by the machine, her life violently extinguished as she "knelt" (138) in the road, her "blood" mingling with the "dust." The religious suggestion behind this scene is continued later when his friend Michaelis queries Wilson about his plans:

> "Have you got a church you go to sometimes, George? Maybe even if you haven't been there for a long time? Maybe I could call up the church and get a priest to come over and he could talk to you, see?"
>
> "Don't belong to any."
>
> "You ought to have a church, George, for times like this. You must have gone to a church once. Didn't you get married in a church?" . . .
>
> "That was a long time ago." (158)

Whatever God gave Wilson's life meaning was there "a long time ago." Nothing wondrous-incarnate energizes his step as it did Gatsby's; no intensity of vision emblazes his day; no sense of reckless possibility takes him to a Platonic realm beyond himself. When he fixes upon murdering the person who killed Myrtle, his "glazed eyes turned out to the ashheaps" (160). There they meet the blind eyes of T. J. Eckleburg, before whom George made Myrtle stand in a kind of inverted religious rite when he accused her of adultery:

> "I spoke to her," he muttered, after a long silence. "I told her she might fool me but she couldn't fool God. I took her to the window"—with

an effort he got up and walked to the rear window and leaned with his face pressed against it—"and I said 'God knows what you've been doing, everything you've been doing. You may fool me, but you can't fool God!'"

Standing behind him, Michaelis saw with a shock that he was looking at the eyes of Doctor T. J. Eckleburg, which had just emerged, pale and enormous, from the dissolving night.

"God sees everything," repeated Wilson. (160)

Wilson then goes out and kills the wrong man. Not only is God blind but Wilson, his agent, is blind as well, and Wilson becomes an incarnate inversion of Gatsby. If Gatsby is a son of God in one sense, Wilson becomes a son of God in another. Gatsby sees the world in a wondrous way when he becomes a son of God; Wilson sees the world blindly when he looks into the eyes of T. J. Eckleburg. Gatsby's unlimited sense of possibility took him to the doorstep of heaven; Wilson's sense of hopelessness takes him to the novel's hell. As Wilson moves ponderously and blindly from the valley of ashes, to Tom's house on East Egg, to Gatsby's on West Egg, he carries death with him. Pale of face, with yellow strawlike hair, he seems to leave a trail of ashes behind him, to leave behind, that is, the death of possibility, the death of godlike vision. In this context, it is significant that he arrives in West Egg at 2:30 P.M. At 2:00 Gatsby went for the first swim in his pool that summer, Gatsby who had "hosted" (the word is repeatedly Fitzgerald's) so many parties that season, Gatsby who had stretched his hands toward the green light on Daisy's dock as if reaching for the "grail."

The religious intensity that inhered in Gatsby's imagination had at this moment begun to dim. He had lived "too long with a single dream" to sustain the godlike vision, and his sense of wonder could no longer infuse matter with a reality it didn't have (162). The wondrous vision gives way to the grotesque, promises to defeat, hope to hopelessness. What we have here is the death not of God but of a godlike mentality. Without the sense of eternal possibility, Gatsby will no longer be his own god, will no longer be Gatsby. He will instead be Wilson, consigned to an equally dubious valley of ashes. It is thus symbolically appropriate that Wilson, the blind agent of a blind god—a kind of agent from hell—emerges from the valley of ashes, emerges as an "ashen, fantastic figure," and murders Gatsby at 3:00 P.M., the hour another man-god had died. That Wilson, the agent of the valley of ashes, should also be the agent of Gatsby's death brings the son-of-God theme full circle, for Gatsby, as we shall see, was no more discerning than was Wilson in what he took with such divine intensity unto himself. Gatsby's sense of godlike possibility was equally misdirected. Blindness and power—and ultimately blind power—rule both the heights and the depths of Fitzgerald's narrative world. What Father Schwartz never seems to have told Rudolph Miller, Gatsby's alter ego, is that one must be very careful when one purports to become a son of God, when one takes unto himself the notion of pure possibility, because the gods we create ultimately take power over us.

6

His Father's Business

DAN CODY

he must be about His Father's business, the service of a vast, vulgar, and meretricious beauty. (99)

When Gatsby is seventeen years old, Dan Cody comes sailing into his world. Cody is at that point fifty years old, "a product of the Nevada silver fields, of the Yukon, of every rush for metal since seventy-five." His dealings in Montana copper "made him many times a millionaire" (100). Overwhelmed by Cody's vitality, his lavish and extravagant ways, his splendid yacht *Tuolomee*, Gatsby surrenders a sense of self to, and models himself on, Cody; it is Cody's meretricious business that he attends to for five years before he is cheated out of his bequeathment by Cody's mistress, Ella Kaye. The name Dan Cody is a composite of names that embody the beginning and end of the American frontier.[10] The Christian name suggests Daniel Boone, one of the first pioneers to enter the American wilderness; and the surname suggests William (Buffalo Bill) Cody, the last of the pioneers.

Daniel Boone (1734–1820) was born in Berks County, Pennsylvania, and taken to the Yadkin Valley of North Carolina by his Quaker parents. In May 1769 he ventured into Kentucky, crossing through the Cumberland Gap and for two years explored, mostly alone, the region of central Kentucky. In 1773 he brought his family to Kentucky and, despite attacks from the Indians, helped construct Fort Boonesboro to settle the region. In September 1799 he moved his family further west to Missouri, where he trapped and hunted for the next twenty years.

William (Buffalo Bill) Cody picked up where Boone left off. He was born in Le Claire, Scott County, Iowa, but his family moved in 1854 to Kansas when the Kansas Territory was opened, settling in Salt Creek Valley, near Fort Leavenworth. Cody began his career as a rider for the pony express. When the Civil War reached the territory, he served in the Seventh Kansas Volunteer Cavalry as a teamster. In 1867–68 he supplied buffalo meat to the construction workers on the Union Pacific Railroad (hence his nickname). From 1868 to 1872 he was chief scout for the Fifth United States Cavalry, which was involved in a series of Indian fights, including the defeat of the Cheyenne in 1869. In that year Edward Zane Carroll Judson, a popular author who wrote under the name of Ned Buntline, made Cody the hero of one of his dime novels—a novel later dramatized. After Buntline persuaded Cody to appear in a melodrama in Chicago, Cody remained on the stage for eleven years. Cody's commercial fame was increasing: he was the subject for Prentiss Ingraham and nineteen other dime novelists before, in 1883, he organized his Buffalo Bill's Wild West Show and traveled across America to Europe, dramatizing his version of the Western scene, even appearing in 1887 before Queen Victoria at her Jubilee. In 1893 he was a big success at the Chicago World's Columbian Exposition as he would be in Madison Square Garden, New York City. Hence it was Daniel Boone who entered the wilderness and Buffalo Bill Cody who eventually came out, turning the original experience into fictional form before commercializing it totally in his traveling shows. Cody's later career was testimony to the death of the frontier long before Frederick Jackson Turner delivered his famous paper carrying that thesis.

Daniel Boone and Buffalo Bill Cody are only two of a number of references that suggest the beginning and end of the American frontier in *The Great Gatsby*. When Gatsby's real father appears for Gatsby's funeral, he brings us the information that if Gatsby had lived he would have been another James J. Hill. "He'd of helped build up the country," Mr. Gatz tells us (169). James J. Hill (1838–1916) was a Canadian, born at Rockwood, Ontario, who settled in 1865 in St. Paul, where he began as a freight agent for the Northwest Packet Company and the St. Paul and Pacific Railroad. He eventually bought into the bankrupt railroad and put it on its feet by building new rails and increasing traffic between St. Paul, the Red River Valley, and Winnipeg. In association with other financiers, he bought up the railroad's bonds, renamed it the Great Northern Railway in 1890, and pushed it across the country, reaching Puget Sound in 1893. At this time he also acquired the Northern Pacific and later the Burlington, purchasing the latter in spite of opposition from Edward H. Harriman, head of the Union Pacific. By the end of the century Hill virtually controlled rail traffic in the Northwest. He added to his immense fortune by acquiring on behalf of the Great Northern stockholders the Mesabi iron range, the chief source of iron ore in America up until World War II.

Mr. Gatz also brings with him a well-read copy of *Hopalong Cassidy*, on the back flyleaf of which Gatsby has written his Benjamin Franklin–like resolves. Hopalong Cassidy was the creation of Clarence E. Mulford (1883–1956), who was born in Strator, Illinois, moved with his family to Utica, New York, and later on his own to Brooklyn, where he wrote a series of stories about the Bar 20 Ranch for Caspar Whitney's *Outing Magazine*. In 1907 these stories were collected into the book *Bar 20*, and Hopalong Cassidy was born. Modeled on Wild Bill Hickok and John Wesley Hardin, Cassidy was a Texas rancher who was shot in the leg in a gunfight (hence his name). The *Bar 20* novel was so popular that it gave rise to many others: *The Orphan* (1908), *Hopalong Cassidy* (1910), *Bar 20 Days* (1911), and *The Coming of Cassidy* (1913); eventually there would be twenty-eight in this series alone. Mulford would go on to write more than one hundred western novels and short stories.

Curiously, Gatsby has dated his copy of *Hopalong Cassidy* 12 September 1906, an impossibility since the novel was not published until 1910. Gatsby, who is thirty-two when the action of *The Great Gatsby* takes place in 1922, would have been twenty years old when the novel appeared in 1910—too old to be reading such books—but he would have been sixteen if he had read the novel in 1906. Fitzgerald, who was fourteen when *Hopalong Cassidy* was published, let the error stand because the Mulford book fitted exactly the message that he wanted to carry—

namely, that when Gatsby was reading about the frontier early in the twentieth century, the frontier was already exhausted.

Fitzgerald was reworking a thesis here that had received attention in an important critical book, Van Wyck Brooks's *The Ordeal of Mark Twain* (1922). Brooks had previously argued in *The Wine of the Puritans* (1911) that American culture had really split in two. The aroma of Puritan wine had given rise to transcendentalism, while the substance of the wine had given rise to commercialism; America was thus a country that could not reconcile the material with the ideal. George Santayana had extended this thesis, arguing that America produced two realms of being—downtown or the world of commerce (the realm of men) where the money is made, and uptown or the salon (the realm of women) where the money is spent. Brooks had extended this argument even further in his book on Twain, saying that the rugged sense of reality that Twain had brought from the West was gentrified and watered down under the genteel influence of Twain's wife and people like William Dean Howells. A Puritan will had moved west, conquered the land, and then had become transformed by the moneyed and genteel society of the East.

Fitzgerald suggests all of this tropologically by having Gatsby write his Benjamin Franklin–like Puritan resolves into the back flyleaf of a western, thus linking the will of the Puritans with the westward movement—a movement that had come to an end, as suggested by *Hopalong Cassidy,* which had turned the reality of the frontier into the romantic subject of a commercial book. The world of Daniel Boone had long given way—to Buffalo Bill's Wild West Shows and to the James J. Hills, who pushed the Great Northern Railroad to the Pacific coast and stripped the Mosabi range of its ore to feed the industrial furnaces of Pittsburgh. The myth of the lost frontier was now being celebrated by the Clarence E. Mulfords, creating their Hopalong Cassidys from the weak wine of genre fiction without ever having stepped a foot beyond the Mississippi. It is Gatsby who buys into this dream when it is already dead. Gatsby models himself on Dan Cody when the frontiersman is now a relic of an exhausted past, and he brings his western individualism and resolves east, where he finds an equivalent for them in the world of Meyer Wolfsheim, but not in the world of Tom and Daisy

Buchanan, westerners who have given themselves over to the social hierarchies and the formal pretenses of the genteel East, suggested by the imitation Georgian mansion in which they live. The image of self that he brings from the West—like the earthy self that Van Wyck Brooks's Twain also brought from the West—Gatsby is unable to reconcile with the heightened and genteel world of the East, unable also to fulfill an idealized image of self in the crassly material world of Tom Buchanan. America had exhausted the western frontier and the iron resolve that had pushed the frontiersmen across a continent, and the spirit of such activity was no longer in sync with the world of the East. The material undoing of a dream and the conflict between East and West—these will become major themes in Fitzgerald's novel.

References to the West and the frontier begin to accumulate in *The Great Gatsby*. References to Dan Cody, James J. Hill, Hopalong Cassidy—all create a kind of subliminal commentary on the differences between East and West; what we finally have in this novel is an almost perfect example of the inverted western. The traditional western grows out of the conflict between civilization (usually embodied by a city) and the wilderness (usually embodied by the idea of the West). A man is tested against nature and then tested again by how well he behaves in relation to other men. As men of courage and initiative found themselves frustrated in the East, controlled by political and financial institutions, they moved West, confronted the land, imposed their will upon that land, and turned that control into landed wealth. Out of this pattern came the myth of the cowboy, played in films by such larger-than-life-figures as Gary Cooper and John Wayne, and sometimes staged politically by such equally theatrical figures as Lyndon Johnson and Ronald Reagan. The origins of this prototype go back to James Fenimore Cooper's Natty Bumppo and Mark Twain's Huckleberry Finn, who became the basis for a new "pop" version of this hero in the writing of Owen Wister, who published his famous western, *The Virginian,* in 1902 and who, like Fenimore Cooper before him, created out of his imagination a West he never knew. As the title suggests, Wister's hero is a Virginian who brings the chivalric and courtly values of the South to the West. He also brings west the values of another Virginian, Thomas

Jefferson, especially the Jeffersonian belief in an aristocracy based on yeoman work and on landed values. In Wyoming the Virginian dedicates himself to these ideals, especially as they are expressed by Judge Henry, whose will he embodies. In the course of time he falls in love with Molly Wood, the schoolteacher, also from the East, who embodies a desire for domesticity. When the Virginian is injured, she nurses him back to health. At the moment they intend to marry their plans are frustrated by the challenge from the novel's villain, Trampas, who not only embodies the opposite of courtly values, but also challenges the very idea of a new, western aristocracy based on agrarian values and natural ability. Trampas's challenge is also to the Virginian's male courage. Thus all of the novel's principal values are challenged by Trampas, whom the Virginian must defeat in personal confrontation, man against man. That the Virginian triumphs surprises no one; that all the values are restored by this triumph also goes without saying; and that the Virginian sets roots in the West with the hope of a new and fulfilling way of life was the reassuring message of the novel.

The Great Gatsby inverts this narrative pattern. Instead of creating himself in the East and going west, Gatsby creates himself in the West and goes east. Instead of bringing a kind of Jeffersonian idealism East, he brings with him the last vestiges of frontier rowdyism. Instead of challenging the open land in the name of self, Gatsby challenges the city in the name of self. Instead of becoming the will of Justice Henry, he becomes an extension of Meyer Wolfsheim. Like the Virginian, Gatsby falls in love, and when he is about to realize that love, he also is confronted by the novel's "villain," Tom Buchanan, who embodies all that Gatsby does not. The scene in the Plaza Hotel in chapter 7 involving the confrontation between Gatsby and Tom is the eastern equivalent of the western shoot-out. But instead of winning the shoot-out, as does the Virginian, Gatsby loses, as he is bound to once he ends up playing Tom's game. Unlike *The Virginian, The Great Gatsby* does not recuperate the hero's ideals. Gatsby is killed, Daisy returns to Tom, and the values of the hero turn out to be a grand illusion. The rest is left to the narrator, Nick Carraway, who at the end returns to the West, reasserting what is left of the value system the novel has just undone.

The allusions and narrative meaning built into *The Great Gatsby* recapitulate the history of the American frontier. That history was codified long after it was a lived experience in the popular genre of the western novel. That history was told in still a different form by Frederick Jackson Turner in his famous frontier thesis, *The Frontier in American History.*

Based upon his analysis of the 1890 census reports, Turner maintained in 1893 that the frontier was already closed. Trained at Johns Hopkins University and teaching at the University of Wisconsin (his native state), Turner challenged the very idea of the old history that located historical meaning in political and economic institutions and that saw the development of America as an extension of European ideas that were brought to America, institutionalized in the East, where they then pervaded America. Turner defined the frontier as that realm that "lies at the hither edge of free land. In the census report it is treated as the margin of that settlement which has a density of two or more to the square mile." Such a frontier, Turner maintained, defined America. The colonist became a new species when he entered the frontier. "The wilderness master[ed] the colonist," Turner claimed. His European trappings were stripped from him, so also were "the garments of civilization." He found himself in hunting shirt, moccasins, and log cabin, planting Indian corn and plowing with a sharp stick. He was transformed by the frontier before he transformed it. The outcome was "not the old Europe. . . . The fact is, that here is a new product that is American."[11] America hence became an end product of the frontier: "It was this nationalizing tendency of the West that transformed the democracy of Jefferson into the national republicanism of Monroe and the democracy of Andrew Jackson" (Turner, 14).

For Turner the frontier embodied that sense of wonder that is inseparable from America. With it came a new sense of hope, an engendering of desire where the process of expectation was more important than deeds of fulfillment. The romantic emotion Nick calls up at the end of the novel is different only in rhetorical intensity from the same emotion that Turner gives us at the end of his famous essay:

His Father's Business

Since the days when the fleet of Columbus sailed into the waters of the New World, America has been another name for opportunity, and the people of the United States have taken their tone from the incessant expansion which has not only been open but has even been forced upon them . . . never again will such gifts of free land offer themselves. For a moment, at the frontier, the bonds of custom are broken and unrestraint is triumphant. . . . And now, four centuries from the discovery of America, at the end of a hundred years of life under the Constitution, the frontier has gone, and with its going has closed the first period of American History. (Turner, 18)

Like Nick Carraway in *The Great Gatsby* Turner locates an idealized America in the dead Jeffersonian past. With the end of the frontier the city becomes the new nexus of power. The ending of *Gatsby* registers each of these ideas. Nick tells us that Gatsby's dream is dead, that it "was already behind him . . . in that vast obscurity beyond the city"—that is, "before" the rise of the city and "beyond" it in the frontier. There "the dark fields of the republic"—that is, the lost hope of Jefferson—"rolled on under the night" (182). This hope was embodied for the Dutch sailors by the "green breast of the new world," and for Gatsby by the "green light" on Daisy's dock. This is the "orgiastic future" ("orgastic" in the first edition) that eludes us all at the same time that it keeps us running, keeps us beating on, "boats against the current, borne back ceaselessly into the past" (182).

In different ways, both Turner and Fitzgerald were suggesting that with the end of the frontier—and with the rise of the new city—the dynamics of progressive history were shifting along sectional lines, particularly in terms of the difference between East and West. And it is precisely to this point that Nick returns in the last pages of the novel when he deliberately and effectively contrasts what the East and the West now mean to him. Like Turner, he finds the provincialism of the West reassuring, while the anonymity of the East is deeply disturbing. In two passages that are meant to be read in juxtaposition with each other, Nick tells us that he connects the West with homes that have been passed down from one generation to the next and are known by their family names—names like the Ordways, Herseys, Schultzes—as well as the Carraways. These homes

(the names of which contrast with the names of the people who attended
Gatsby's parties) are further connected in Nick's mind with his memory
of Christmas returns home to Minnesota, with fields of snow and small
Wisconsin stations seen from train windows, and with street lamps and
sleigh bells and frosted breath and holly wreaths in lighted windows. The
comforts of the West dissolve into a kind of nightmarish dream of the
East, a dream that gives embodiment to the kind of drunken impersonal-
ity that Nick witnessed at Gatsby's parties and at the trysting house
where Tom takes Myrtle Wilson. Such a scene, Nick tells us, could be
out of El Greco:

> a hundred houses, at once conventional and grotesque, crouching
> under a sullen, overhanging sky and a lustreless moon. In the fore-
> ground four solemn men in dress suits are walking along the sidewalk
> with a stretcher on which lies a drunken woman in a white evening
> dress. Her hand, which dangles over the side, sparkles cold with jewels.
> Gravely the men turn in at a house—the wrong house. But no one
> knows the woman's name, and no one cares. (178)

Houses that bear family names give way to mistaken realms that
house the nameless. *The Great Gatsby* in some ways is a story of homes—
and of seasons. The scenes in the East take place mostly in summer, and
Nick's memory of the West is that of winter; but the East is cold, and the
West brings with it a sense of warmth. "This has been a story of the
West," Nick tells us (177). But it has also been a story of the East. Behind
the idea of the East is a sense of fixed money, of institutional power, of
class differences, of the anonymity of the megalopolis. Behind the idea of
the West is a sense of mobility, of new opportunity, of a personal and
human scale. The western experiences Nick connects with the realm of
his childhood, the eastern experiences with what he has witnessed in the
summer of 1922. Nick endows the West and not the East with a moral
center. That such a moral center is located in the past of his adolescence
is an irony seldom commented upon by critics. In returning to the safe
world of his lost childhood is Nick also going in search of the ideal located in the dead past? Or is Fitzgerald telling us that it is the fate of every

American to pursue ideals only when they are already exhausted of meaning? We shall return to these questions in another context. It remains here only to point out that when Gatsby takes to the East the embodiment of the self that he created in the West, we have in effect an inverted western at work. Once Gatsby begins to go about Dan Cody's business in the realm that has replaced the frontier, he indeed goes in pursuit of meretricious beauty.

MEYER WOLFSHEIM

"I raised him up out of nothing, right out of the gutter." (172)

When Gatsby was discharged from the army, he went to New York, where he met Meyer Wolfsheim in Weinbrenner's poolroom on Forty-third Street. Gatsby was so hard up at this time, Wolfsheim tells us, that he was still wearing his army uniform and had not eaten for "a couple of days." When Wolfsheim learns that Gatsby is an army hero with Oxford "gonnegtions," he realizes that he can use him as a front man in his illegal operations. "I got him to join up in the American Legion and he used to stand high there," Wolfsheim tells Nick. "Right off he did some work for a client of mine up to Albany" (172).

Meyer Wolfsheim, we in turn discover, is the man who "fixed" the World Series in 1919. The very idea challenges the provincial faith that Nick has in the American system:

> The idea staggered me. I remembered, of course, that the World's Series had been fixed in 1919, but if I had thought of it at all I would have thought of it as a thing that merely *happened*, the end of some inevitable chain. It never occurred to me that one man could start to play with the faith of fifty million people—with the single-mindedness of a burglar blowing a safe. (74)

The reference to the fixed World Series of 1919 links Arnold Rothstein with Fitzgerald's Meyer Wolfsheim. Rothstein had become king of the

New York bookmakers, the proprietor of a big gambling hotel, and the owner of a profitable racing stable. He was also very much involved in New York bootlegging and in fraudulent brokerage houses. Rothstein had not actually fixed the World Series of 1919, although his name was connected with the setup that led the Chicago White Sox to lose to Cincinnati. At that time the White Sox were owned by Charles Comiskey, one of the founders of the American League. A reserve clause kept all ballplayers bound to the one team with which they had signed. Comiskey used this regulation to keep wages low, mostly at the big-league minimum of $2,500. When his players negotiated for raises, they were refused, despite the fact that Chicago had one of the best teams in baseball. In disgust, a number of players thought up the idea of throwing the World Series. Eddie Cicotte, the team's leading pitcher, and Chick Gandil, the first baseman, contacted Joseph "Sport" Sullivan, the biggest gambler in Boston, and agreed to lose to Cincinnati if the ten players involved were paid $10,000 for throwing the series. Sullivan, who liked the deal, did not have the $100,000 to back it, but he suggested that Arnold Rothstein might put up the money. As the first game approached, Cicotte, who could not get confirmation from Sullivan, contacted Bill Burns, a former baseball player who gambled heavily with a fortune he had made in the oil business. Burns also was interested in the deal but, like Sullivan, refused to put up $100,000. He too suggested Rothstein as a possible backer and sent William Maharg, a former boxer, to get Rothstein's response. Rothstein, who met Maharg at the Astor Hotel, refused to get involved because he believed too many people were aware of the deal and because he was suspicious of Maharg, whom he didn't know. But Maharg claims that he was later told by Burns that Rothstein had changed his mind and was coming in on the deal once he had been contacted by Abe Attell, another fighter, whom Rothstein knew personally.

Attell began to take bets in great quantity in the lobby of the Sinton Hotel in Cincinnati and elsewhere. When the players asked for money up front, Attell refused, but said that he would give them $20,000 after each game they lost, up to $100,000, since in 1919 the series was played until one team won five games. After the White Sox lost the first game,

Maharg came for the players' money. In a room overflowing with money, Attell refused to give the players the agreed-upon $20,000, and said that he would pay them at the end of the series. The players were now in so deeply that they were forced to throw the series. Although Rothstein's name was closely connected with the fix, Rothstein maintained that Attell had merely used his name to get the players involved and that he had never agreed to the deal—indeed, that he had turned Maharg down when contacted. But later evidence indicates that Rothstein may have been using Attell, rather than the other way around. Although cautious, Rothstein knew of the players' situation and seemed to bet warily, game to game, on Cincinnati. He later maintained that he won less than $100,000 on the series, but others fix the sum at about $350,000. Even to this day Rothstein's role in the fixed series is vague. When Nick asks Gatsby why Wolfshcim is not in jail, Gatsby responds with words that were equally true of Rothstein: "They can't get him, old sport. He's a smart man."[12]

Fitzgerald lived in New York from February to July 1919 and October 1920 to July 1921 and again on Long Island from October 1923 to April 1924, where he began writing *The Great Gatsby*. During this time— probably in 1923 or 1924—he met Rothstein, an event he later recalled as having a strong influence on his novel:

> [I]n *Gatsby* I selected the stuff to fit a given mood or "hauntedness" or whatever you might call it, rejecting in advance in *Gatsby*, for instance, all of the ordinary material for Long Island, big crooks, adultery theme and always starting from the *small* focal point that impressed me—my own meeting with Arnold Rothstein for instance.[13]

Fitzgerald most likely met Rothstein the way that Nick met Wolfsheim —in this case through his Great Neck neighbor named Edward Fuller. In a letter to Maxwell Perkins from Europe (ca. 20 December 1924) Fitzgerald wrote that "after careful searching of the files (of a man's mind here) for the Fuller Magee [*sic*] case and after having had Zelda draw pictures until her fingers ache I know Gatsby better than I know my own child" (*Letters*, 173).

At the time that Fitzgerald knew Edward Fuller, Fuller and later his partner, William McGee (Fitzgerald had misspelled McGee's name in his letter to Perkins), were being indicted on charges of fraudulent stock dealing. According to the *New York Times* (14 November 1922):

> The examination of witnesses at the trial of Edward M. Fuller of the bankrupt firm of E. M. Fuller and Co. will begin today in General Sessions. William F. McGee, a co-defendant with Fuller, on an indictment charging bucketing of orders, will have a separate trial. The jury in the Fuller's case was completed yesterday. (31, col. 2)

The case came about when Franklin B. Link of Westmoreland, Tennessee, charged Fuller and McGee with bucketing his order for $1,500 worth of Middle States Oil stock. At this point, Fuller and McGee declared bankruptcy. After an examination of the firm's books, the liabilities of Fuller and McGee were first set at five million dollars and later at slightly less than two million ($1,888,812).

The Fuller-McGee scheme seems to have worked this way: A. J. Harold Braid, of the brokerage firm of Braid and Vogel on the New York Exchange, allowed his name to be used in making stock transactions for which he received two dollars per share of business. An Albert Biehman, a clerk for Fuller and McGee, would take the prices of stock from the ticker tape, quote the prices to customers, take the customers' orders, but never make the transactions to a broker, "bucketing" the money for Fuller and McGee.

This practice was not new. Since 1917 scores of brokerage firms had gone bankrupt in New York with liabilities of more than $150 million. These companies would sell stock on worthless businesses—especially mineral mines. As long as such "mines" existed and people were willing to buy their stock, this was not illegal. These same brokerage firms, however, often accepted money on legitimate stock and then "bucketed"—that is, pocketed—the money and never completed the customer's order.

The four trials of Fuller and McGee were a series of farces. The first trial resulted in a hung jury. The second was declared a mistrial because J. Harold Braid, the state's principal witness, disappeared. The third

trial—in which four witnesses and important documents disappeared—
also resulted in a hung verdict, the grand jury later investigating attempts
to bribe one of the jurors. The fourth trial, which resulted in the conviction of Fuller and McGee, brought Arnold Rothstein onto the stage
when it was learned that Rothstein had "borrowed" $187,000 from
Edward Fuller. Later investigation showed that Rothstein was the man
behind Fuller and McGee from the very beginning.

When the warrants were first issued, and Fuller and McGee were
charged with "bucketing," they could not be found. Arthur Garfield
Hays, in his *City Lawyer,* describes how he was summoned to assist Fuller
and McGee:

> After the bankruptcy of E. M. Fuller and Company, the assets, Fuller,
> and McGee all vanished. A few weeks later a telephone call summoned
> me to a brownstone house on the upper West Side. I asked who lived
> there. "Arnold Rothstein." . . . Fuller and McGee were comfortably
> living in Rothstein's home, waiting for the storm to subside. They were
> expecting Bill Fallon [another attorney] that afternoon.[14]

Fitzgerald knew both Rothstein and Fuller, and there is in *The Great
Gatsby* the same relationship between Meyer Wolfsheim and his lieutenant, Jay Gatsby, as there was in real life between Rothstein and his lieutenant, Edward Fuller. When Fitzgerald said that Gatsby "started as one
man I knew and then changed into myself" (*Letters*, 358), that man was
Edward Fuller, Fitzgerald's Great Neck neighbor (just as Nick is Gatsby's
West Egg neighbor).

Fitzgerald could depict Gatsby (Fuller) as a bootlegger, since
Rothstein (Wolfsheim) controlled New York bootlegging. But Gatsby is
more than a bootlegger—and Fitzgerald makes it clear that Gatsby, like
Edward Fuller, was in the bond business. When Gatsby asks Nick to arrange the meeting with Daisy, he suggests that he can help Nick who is
also selling bonds:

> "I carry on a little business on the side, a sort of side line, you under-
> stand. And I thought that if you don't make very much—You're selling
> bonds, aren't you, old sport?"

"Trying to."

"Well, this would interest you. It wouldn't take up much of your time and you might pick up a nice bit of money. It happens to be a rather confidential sort of thing." (83)

When Tom confronts Gatsby at the Plaza Hotel, he insinuates that Gatsby's business is more than just bootlegging. "'That drug-store business was just small change,' continued Tom slowly, 'but you've got something on now that Walter's afraid to tell me about'" (135). And when Nick answers the phone, after Gatsby's death, the unsuspecting caller tells him:

"Young Parke's in trouble," he said rapidly. "They picked him up when he handed the bonds over the counter. They got a circular from New York giving 'em the numbers just five minutes before. What d'you know about that, hey? You never can tell in these hick towns—" [one may recall at this point Gatsby's phone conversations about small towns]. (167)

Meyer Wolfsheim becomes Gatsby's second father figure and introduces him to the New York underworld. It is thus with money that comes from bootlegging, gambling, and bucket shops that Gatsby makes the fortune that allows him to buy his mansion on West Egg. When Nick confronts Wolfsheim after Gatsby's death, he asks him if he had started Gatsby in business:

"Start him! I made him."

"Oh."

"I raised him up out of nothing, right out of the gutter." (172)

The last sentence suggests the exchange in Dickens's *Great Expectations* when Abel Magwitch tells Pip, "Yes, Pip, dear boy, I've made a gentleman on you! It's me wot has done it!"[15] That information shatters Pip's sense of self, since he had all along believed that the money that had made him a gentleman had come from Miss Havisham. When he learns that he owes his rise to a felon's money, he comes to think of both the money and himself as counterfeit. Gatsby never has such compunctions. To him money is money, and he never understands the difference between East Egg and West Egg—the former the home of the established wealth, the latter of the new rich or, like himself, the ersatz and criminally rich. That is why Daisy is "appalled by West Egg, this unprecedented 'place' that Broadway had begotten upon a Long Island fishing village— appalled by its raw vigor . . . and by the too obtrusive fate that herded its inhabitants along a short-cut from nothing to nothing. She saw something awful in the very simplicity she failed to understand" (108).

Once Daisy comes to understand the source of Gatsby's money, her interest in him is gone forever. Gatsby never realizes how tenuous his relationship with Daisy really is, how much it depends not just on money but the right kind of money. He never comes to understand what West Egg stands for or how it is an extension of the city's underworld. As a Westerner, he has brought a frontier sense of self to New York and played it out destructively in the world of Tom Buchanan—that is, the world of the city whose function it is to process money. This is the city that Nick has seen in his ride in from Long Island with Gatsby "rising up across the river in white heaps and sugar lumps all built with a wish out of non-olfactory money" (69). Whatever the "wish," it was not strong enough, and Nick knows that the odor of some money is worse than that of other money. When Tom tells Daisy and Jordan the source of Gatsby's money in the Plaza Hotel scene, Daisy becomes "terrified" and Jordan, "who had begun to balance an invisible but absorbing object on the tip of her chin" (135), simply looked as if something smelled bad, the same way Daisy's chauffeur looked when he had to drive into West Egg (cf. 86). Dan Cody's money was also "olfactory," so also the Buchanans' until it had been "cleansed" over a number of generations by circulating through proper money institutions, buying mansions with the proper address, and financing children through Yale. Gatsby never learns this simple truth because he is too busy being a son of God, too busy going "about His Father's business, the service of a vast, vulgar, and meretricious beauty" (99)—that is, too busy going about the business of America.

7

Inventing Gatsby

So he invented just the sort of Jay Gatsby that a seventeen-year-old boy
would be likely to invent, and to this conception he was faithful to the
end. (99)

At one point in his story of Gatsby, Nick tells us that "if personality is an
unbroken series of successful gestures, then there was something gorgeous about him, some heightened sensitivity to the promises of life" (2).
Fitzgerald's language, as always, is carefully chosen, especially the word
"personality." In his early work Fitzgerald distinguished between the
"egoist" and the "personage." The egoist relied on personality, which de-
pended upon appearance, grooming, gesture—the surface aspects of self.
Personage moves beyond personality to a more essential form of self—
self as process, an accumulated sense of what one can become. These
terms take their meaning from each other; the creation of an essential self
demands the personality through which it is expressed.

Beyond the accidents of personality, we have Gatsby modeling himself on Dan Cody and, of course, having Daisy Fay for his wife. That the
adolescent imagination makes something more "gorgeous" than convinc-
ing out of this notion of self is not surprising. With no real sense of the
differences in class or between kinds of money, with no formal education, with not the faintest idea of how the established rich live and act,
Gatsby sets out to give personality—"gesture" as Nick calls it—to the
personage he has created. The "gestures," of course, include the pink

suits, the silver shirts, the gold ties, the Rolls-Royce swollen with chrome and hat boxes, the clipped speech, the "old sports," the formal intensity of manner, the gracefulness on the ballroom floor, the bending slightly forward in conversation to create the impression of an intensity of interest, the meticulous attention to detail—these and many more "gestures" complement the personage of Gatsby. Of course, the pretensions to an Oxford education seem totally out of context with this sense of self—as indeed they are. Beneath the elaborate, albeit gaudy, elegance of Gatsby looms James Gatz, the original "roughneck" that Gatsby spends so much energy trying to conceal. Nick spots the contradictions the first time he meets Gatsby:

> He smiled understandingly—much more than understandingly. It was one of those rare smiles with a quality of eternal reassurance in it, that you may come across four or five times in life. It faced—or seemed to face—the whole external world for an instant, and then concentrated on *you* with an irresistible prejudice in your favor. It understood you just as far as you wanted to be understood, believed in you as you would like to believe in yourself, and assured you that it had precisely the impression of you that, at your best, you hoped to convey. Precisely at that point it vanished—and I was looking at an elegant young roughneck, a year or two over thirty, whose elaborate formality of speech just missed being absurd. (48)

Gatsby does not quite bring it off, and the contradictions call attention to the seam between what he tries to be as a personage and what he is as a personality. In the ride from West Egg to Manhattan, Gatsby recites for Nick the essential self that he has created: "'I am the son of some wealthy people in the Middle West—all dead now. I was brought up in America but educated at Oxford, because all my ancestors have been educated there for many years. It is a family tradition'" (65). Like Jordan Baker, Nick does not believe him, and comes to understand why so many of Gatsby's guests feel that there is something sinister about him:

> He looked at me sideways—and I knew why Jordan Baker had believed he was lying. He hurried the phrase "educated at Oxford," or

swallowed it, or choked on it, as though it had bothered him before. And with this doubt, his whole statement fell to pieces, and I wondered if there wasn't something a little sinister about him, after all. (65)

Gatsby begins with an element of truth (he did go to Oxford briefly after the war on a government scholarship) and then gives way to total distortion. Gatsby hardly comes from Midwest wealth or a tradition of genteel breeding connected with an Oxford education. When Nick asks him where in the Midwest he comes from, Gatsby ignorantly, but elegantly, tells him San Francisco, geography losing to the pretensions of the romantic imagination. The more Gatsby talks the more absurd his story becomes. Nick believes "that he was pulling my leg" until "a glance at him convinced me otherwise." "After that," Gatsby continues, "I lived like a young rajah in all the capitals of Europe—Paris, Venice, Rome— collecting jewels, chiefly rubies, hunting big game, painting a little, things for myself only, and trying to forget something very sad that happened to me long ago" (66). By this point Nick can hardly control his "incredulous laughter." Although well rehearsed, Gatsby's story is so romantically exaggerated—and so historically untrue—that Nick has the image of a "turbaned 'character' leaking sawdust at every pore as he pursued a tiger through the Bois de Boulogne" (66). What is happening here on the level of rhetoric will have its parallel on the level of plot because it is Gatsby's inability to bring his romantic conception of self in sync with historical reality that leads to his destruction.

The intensity of vision has little basis in reality, and it is exactly this intensity that sustains Gatsby's love for Daisy Fay. As Nick tells us, "the vitality of his illusion" went "beyond her, beyond everything. He had thrown himself into it with a creative passion, adding to it all the time" (97). What Fitzgerald is working with here is the romantic vision. At one point in the novel, Daisy tells us that "it's very romantic outdoors" because there is a bird on her lawn that "must be a nightingale come over on the Cunard or White Star Line" (16). The allusion evokes the poetry of Keats, which Fitzgerald knew well and which he integrated into many of his major works, especially *Tender is the Night*, which takes its title from a line by Keats. Fitzgerald had studied the romantic poets with Christian

Gauss at Princeton, and when his daughter was in college, Fitzgerald remembered that experience:

> "The Grecian Urn" is unbearably beautiful with every syllable as inevitable as the notes in Beethoven's Ninth Symphony. . . . I suppose I've read it a hundred times. About the tenth time I began to know what it was about, and caught the chime in it and the exquisite inner mechanics. Likewise with "The Nightingale" which I can never read through without tears in my eyes; likewise the "Pot of Basil" ["Isabella"] with its great stanzas about the two brothers, "Why were they proud, etc."; and "The Eve of St. Agnes," which has the richest, most sensuous imagery in English, not excepting Shakespeare. And finally his three or four great sonnets, "Bright Star" and the others (*Letters*, 88).

It was Keats who once wrote, "there is a space of life between boyhood and maturity in which the soul is in ferment, the characters undecided, the way of life uncertain, the ambition thick-sighted."[16] This is the moment, when the romantic creates himself, that Jay Gatsby came into being. All of Fitzgerald's major characters go through this experience, as a look at his other novels quickly reveals:

> [Amory Blaine, of *This Side of Paradise*] wondered how people could fail to notice that he was a boy marked for glory.

> [Anthony Patch, of *The Beautiful and Damned*] thrilled to remote harmonies . . . for he was young now as he would never be again, and more triumphant than death.

> In the spring of 1917, when Doctor Richard Diver [of *Tender Is the Night*] first arrived in Zurich, he was twenty-six years old, a fine age for a man, indeed, the very acme of bachelorhood . . . [bringing with him] the illusions of eternal strength and health, and of the essential goodness of people; illusions of a nation.

> [Monroe Stahr, of *The Last Tycoon*] had flown up very high to see, on strong wings, when he was young. And while he was up there he had looked on all the kingdoms, with the kind of eyes that can stare straight into the sun.[17]

The romantic unfolding of self is inseparable from the romantic belief that the universe is alive and that fulfillment is a process of growth. The emphasis is on becoming rather than being, on expectation rather than reality. In its most radical form, as Morse Peckham has told us, "dynamic organicism results in the idea that the history of the universe is the history of God creating himself."[18] Thus the true romantic, as we have already seen in the case of Gatsby, is the son of God, repeating the godlike activity of creation. Such activity is not without its dangers. Keats's lovers—Lamia, Endymion, Hyperion—are all destroyed in this way. And when the heroes and heroines are not physically destroyed, they often experience radical disillusionment, become eternal wanderers, alienated from society, outcasts. Such is the fate of Byron's Harold, Manfred, and Cain, and of Shelley's Alastor. They wander between Carlyle's "everlasting yea" and "everlasting no" (or what Peckham calls positive and negative romanticism), seeking new commitment, often in the form of an ideal that is already exhausted. Their mortal enemy is time, ideally embodied in youth—with its romantic commitment and sense of the potential. When time is wasted it brings on romantic sadness; when it is remembered it brings on romantic nostalgia. If the idealized moment gives way to nostalgia in Fitzgerald's fiction, nostalgia in turn gives way to the horror of wasted youth, and it is within these three realms of time—time idealized, time sentimentalized, and time regretted—that Fitzgerald's fiction works.

This narrative pattern can be found repeatedly in romantic and postromantic works, and we know from reading *This Side of Paradise* that Amory Blaine (and presumably Fitzgerald himself) read such works. But one does not have to make an argument based on influence to document narrative parallels. Fitzgerald was breathing romantic air when he wrote, and works like Walter Pater's *Marius the Epicurean* and Ernest Dowson's "The Princess of Dreams" seem long stamped upon his imagination. As with Gatsby, Marius's development involves movement from romantic commitment to romantic disillusionment. Marius passes through four stages of experience: first, his boyhood and school life; then he becomes an Epicurean of the Cyrenaic school, which extols the idea of youth; next he becomes disillusioned with the Cyrenaic philosophy; and finally, he moves on to Christianity, deeply attracted to the aesthetics of the new religion but still without the faith to believe. It is in his second stage of development, his belief in Cyrenaicism, that Marius shares a state of mind with Gatsby:

> Thus the boyhood of Marius passed; on the whole more given to contemplation than to action. Less prosperous in fortune than at an earlier day there had been reason to expect ... he lived much in the realm of the imagination, and became betimes, as he was to continue all through life, something of an idealist, constructing the world for himself in great measure from within, by the exercise of meditative power. ... [He had an] innate and habitual longing for a world altogether fairer than that he saw.[19]

As Gatsby created in his imagination a world that did not exist, Marius does also. And as Gatsby idealizes Daisy Fay so Marius also had "the ideal of a perfect imaginative love, centered upon a type of beauty entirely flawless and clean" (Pater, 76).

If Pater actually catches the romantic process by which a Gatsby comes into being, Ernest Dowson's "The Princess of Dreams," a prose poem, recapitulates the narrative pattern of such a story. Here the hero returns with a newly amassed treasure to a beautiful girl whom he once loved. He fails, however, to regain her love and is defeated at the hands of a cruel and "slow witted" competitor, a guardian of her tower. In a work with astonishing parallels to *The Great Gatsby* the hero disappears and the poem ends with the suggestion that the golden "princess" is fraudulently unworthy of the hero:

> For once in a dream he had seen, as they were flowers de luce, the blue lakes of her eyes, had seemed to be enveloped in a tangle of her golden hair.
> And he sought her through the countless windings of her forest for many moons, sought her through the morasses, sparing not his horse nor his sword.
> Poor legendary princess.
> For he did not free her and the fustian porter took his treasure and broke his stained sword in two. ...

But there are some who say that she had no wish to be freed, and that those flowers de luce, her eyes, are a stagnant, dark pool, that her glorious golden hair was only long enough to reach her postern gate. Some say, moreover, that her tower is not of ivory and that she is not even virtuous nor a princess.[20]

When Fitzgerald was writing *The Great Gatsby* in 1923–24, he was not writing within the same cultural context as Pater and Dowson. What had radically altered the romantic vision in the intervening years was an opposing view that was itself a product of the new science with its belief in the Kingdom of Power, the Dynamics of Force. The play between a belief in romantic commitment and a belief in the limits set by force is at the very heart of modernism, expressed as a dualism between a mechanistic and organic view of the universe. The organic universe is self-contained, capable of growth, is marked by its ability to assimilate diverse material into its own substance, and relies on the spontaneous source of its own energy, as well as the interdependence of parts to parts and of the parts to the whole. The mechanistic universe presupposes a universe made up of matter in motion; such matter obeys physical laws, so that there are no miracles in nature. The organic universe is living, continually unfolding, revealing itself symbolically. The mechanistic universe is fixed, understandable through scientific laws like the law of gravity or thermodynamics, which explain matter, through which force is expressed. In literature the naturalists were trying to reduce reality to mechanistic terms, while the romantics were trying to infuse matter with spirit, energy, and life. H. G. Wells would embody the first position, while D. H. Lawrence would embody the second, and a number of other writers experimented to bridge this kind of division: Joyce, for example, with his "yes" of feminine replenishment, William James with his belief in the need for a religious state of mind that gives matter direction, Samuel Butler with his interest in creative evolution, George Bernard Shaw with his belief in the life force, and Henri Bergson with his theories of vitalism.

Henry Adams took up the argument in America. Built into Adams's vision of the universe, as in Fitzgerald's, was a sense of both systems at work. His belief in the Virgin—in the feminine principle in life, inseparable from a mythic sense of life, and from the unity of an age—revealed a deep sense of the romantic. But his awareness of the Dynamo took him into the realm of force, which, he felt, totally disrupted the possibility of romantic fulfillment. Adams had painfully discovered that history was no longer knowledge but the brute violence of irrational energies. The masculine principle (the Dynamo) had overcome the feminine principle of life (the Virgin); technology, urbanization, the rise of the corporation, and other money institutions had led to the powerhouse of change. As he put it in chapter 25 of *The Education:*

> Satisfied that the sequence of men led to nothing and the sequence of
> their society could lead no further, while the . . . sequence of thought
> was chaos, he turned at last to the sequence of force; and thus it hap-
> pened that, after ten years' pursuit, he found himself lying in the Gal-
> lery of Machines at the Great Exposition of 1900, his historical neck
> broken by the sudden irruption of forces totally new.[21]

"Chaos was the law of nature; order was the dream of man," Adams wrote. Modern technological man had gone beyond nature, had forced his mechanical will on the land, and turned that control into wealth.

What we have here is a modern, American Crusoe, who, like Defoe's prototype, had come to the new world, and then moved across a continent, eliminating the Indian and despoiling the land. Crusoe came after Nick Carraway's Dutch sailors, for whom the new world "flowered," as Daisy flowered for Gatsby (as her very name suggests). Into this world Daniel Boone entered, and out of it came William (Buffalo Bill) Cody. Gatsby embodies the beginning and end of this romantic process; his antagonist, Tom Buchanan, the kingdom of force. Nick Carraway makes the connections between these elements the night Gatsby told him the story of "Dan Cody—told it to me because 'Jay Gatsby' had broken up like glass against Tom's hard malice" (148). The wording here is important. It is not just Jay Gatsby, but also the "idea" of "Jay Gatsby" (as Fitzgerald's quotation marks suggest) that is destroyed by Tom Buchanan. Tom incarnates the new realm of force. The first time we see him Fitzgerald emphasizes this point when Nick tells us, "Not even the effeminate swank of his riding clothes could hide the enormous power of that body—he seemed to fill those glistening boots until he strained the top lacing, and you could see a great pack of muscle shifting when his shoulder moved under his thin coat. It was a body capable of enormous leverage—a cruel body" (7). Tom puts that power to use often. He has hurt Daisy's hand (12), breaks Myrtle's nose (37), and turns Nick around with one arm, at once denying and asserting that "I'm stronger and more of a man than you are" (7).

Such physical force becomes a trope in the novel for the new America—the America in which force is embodied in corporations and in money institutions, embodied in the new urban process, and controlled by finance and the power of information. Tom defeats Gatsby with information by knowing what others do not know. By exposing the origins of Gatsby's money, he overpowers Gatsby's display of self. Although Gatsby created wild discrepancies between what he was as a "personage" and as a "personality," he held, to his credit, that sense of self together by the immense vitality of romantic will. Unfortunately for him, a greater force is at work—a mechanistic force equivalent to the working of the Dynamo, and it is against this force that Gatsby breaks "like glass" (148). In depicting the rise and fall of Gatsby, Fitzgerald not only gave us an insight into the life and death of a romantic hero, but he also gave us an insight into the cultural dynamics of the twentieth century, showing us how Henry Adams picked up where John Keats left off.

8

Careless People: Daisy Fay

They were careless people, Tom and Daisy—they smashed up things and creatures and then retreated back into their money or their vast carelessness, or whatever it was that kept them together, and let other people clean up the mess they had made. (180–81)

In Fitzgerald's fiction the idealized woman becomes the object of romantic obsession. In *The Great Gatsby* the object of such attention is, of course, Daisy Fay. Nick says of Gatsby that "some idea of himself perhaps . . . had gone into loving Daisy" (111). When Gatsby loses Daisy, he loses a sense of self that leaves him "confused and disordered." If he can only regain Daisy, Nick continues, perhaps he could regain that sense of self. The narrative pattern here is a kind of watermark of Fitzgerald's fiction. Stories like "Winter Dreams," "The Last of the Belles," "The Sensible Thing," "Dice, Brassknuckles and Guitar," "Diamond Dick and the First Law of Woman," and "The Third Casket" sustain this theme.

The story was so compelling for Fitzgerald because it was one that he had lived firsthand when his love affair with Ginevra King broke up. Both Isabelle of "Babes in the Woods" and Helen of "The Debutante" are based on Ginevra King as is Rosalind in *This Side of Paradise*. Fitzgerald recorded his love affair with Ginevra in his "Ledger," an informal diary that he kept of the major events in his life, all in a kind of cryptic shorthand: January 1915: "Met Ginevra"; June: "Ritz, Nobody Home and Midnight Follie with Ginevra. . . ." Deering: "I'm going to take Ginevra home in my electric"; August: "No news from Ginevra";

October: "Dinner with Ginevra in Waterbury"; November: "Letters to G. K."; February 1916: "Long letters to Ginevra"; March: "Ginevra fired from school"; April: "Ginevra and Living on the train. A fascinating story"; August: "Lake Forest. Peg Carry. Petting Party. Ginevra. Party"; November: "Ginevra and Margaret Cary to Yale game"; January 1917: "Final break with Ginevra"; June: "Ginevra engaged?"; September: "Oh Ginevra"; July 1918: "Zelda . . . Ginevra married." So deep was Fitzgerald's first love for Ginevra King that fifteen years later he was writing about her in his Josephine stories, and twenty years later, in 1937, he described her again in his story "Between Planes."

Fitzgerald once said that he could not write unless he brought an intensity of emotion to a story. It was the intensity of the Ginevra King experience that he was bringing to *The Great Gatsby*. In a letter to Maxwell Perkins from Rome, dated 20 December 1924, Fitzgerald recounts the creation of *The Great Gatsby*, which he was then in the process of revising. After mentioning Tom Buchanan, Gatsby, Daisy, and Myrtle, he says: "Jordan [Baker] of course was a great idea (perhaps you know it's Edith Cummings)" (*Letters*, 173). Edith Cummings was a close friend of Ginevra King, both in Lake Forest and at the Westover School for Girls, a finishing school in Connecticut where they were both in the class of 1917. Like Jordan Baker, she was a well-known golfer, playing out of the prestigious Onwentsia Club in Chicago, and once winning the national woman's golf championship. Fitzgerald met Edith Cummings a number of times—both in Lake Forest and in New York—when he was dating Ginevra.

Fitzgerald first met Ginevra when she was invited to St. Paul by Marie Hersey. On 4 January 1915 they met at a dinner dance at the Town and Country Club, an event Fitzgerald described in "Babes in the Woods," published in the *Nassau Literary Magazine* (May 1917) and later included in *This Side of Paradise*. The unhappy ending to this love affair he described in "The Debutante," also published in the *Nassau Literary Magazine* (January 1917). The events that took place between these two stories are the ones we find cryptically recounted in the Ledger. In June 1915 they met in New York and went to *Nobody Home* and the Midnight Follie. In March 1916 Ginevra was expelled from Westover by the headmistress, Miss Hillard, an event Fitzgerald recounted fourteen years later in the *Saturday Evening Post* (September 1930) short story "A Woman with a Past," which he later included in *Taps at Reveille.* In this story Josephine is put on probation by a Miss Kwain who maintained that Josephine was flirting with boys calling to her from under her dormitory window. Soon after, while walking with Ernest Waterbury near the campus chapel, Josephine "slipped" into his "unwilling arms, where she lay helpless, convulsed with irresistible laughter. It was in this position that Miss Brereton and the visiting trustee had found them" (*Stories*, 375). Miss Brereton expelled Josephine and then retracted, just as Miss Hillard had expelled Ginevra and then retracted. Neither Ginevra nor Josephine, however, would return to the school.

In August 1916 Fitzgerald visited Ginevra in Lake Forest. Peg Carry, Edith Cummings, Courtney Letts—the old Westover crowd—were all there and, as we have seen in Fitzgerald's Ledger, there was a "petting party" and many romantic evenings. But these events were more casual than sustained. There is no proof that Ginevra took Fitzgerald as seriously as he took her, and there is evidence that the Kings disapproved of Fitzgerald. In his "Ledger" Fitzgerald wrote that someone at this time told him, "Poor boys shouldn't think of marrying rich girls." If Mr. King would not put it this crudely, these were his sentiments.

The next time that Fitzgerald saw Ginevra King was with Peg Carry at the Yale game in November 1916. Ginevra met Fitzgerald once again in January 1917, at which time she broke with him for good. The conclusion of "A Woman with a Past" is thus pure daydream. When Josephine leaves school, she goes to Hot Springs, where she meets a young man who "had flunked out of Princeton in February" (*Stories*, 376). (Fitzgerald had not exactly "flunked out" of Princeton, but the reference is obvious.) Josephine learns at Hot Springs something that Nick Carraway learns in *The Great Gatsby*—that playing with others' affections has moral consequences: "One mustn't run through people . . . for the sake of a romantic half-hour" (*Stories*, 380). The moment she realizes this, she sees Mr. Gordon Tinsley, from Yale, "the current catch of Chicago, reputedly the richest young man in the Middle West. He had never paid any attention to young Josephine until tonight. Ten minutes ago he had asked her to go driving with him." She rejects him because "the Princeton man was still at her ear, still imploring her to walk out with him into the night (*Stories*, 379–80).

It did not happen this way in life. Fitzgerald in June 1917 suspected that Ginevra was engaged; in September he wrote in his Ledger, "Oh Ginevra"; by June 1918, while he was stationed at Camp Sheridan near Montgomery, Alabama, he found out that Ginevra King was to be married on 24 September. She was marrying William Mitchell who, like Gordon Tinsley in the story, was "the current catch of Chicago." Mitchell was from an extremely wealthy family, long associated with Chicago banking, especially with the Continental Illinois Bank. After he married Ginevra, Mitchell became a director in the family firm of Mitchell, Hutchins & Co., and served on the boards of Balaban and Katz, Inland Glass, and Elgin Clock.

Ginevra King's father, like Josephine's father, went to Yale (class of 1894), and Charles King and William Mitchell both owned a string of polo ponies, Mr. King bringing his East to Long Island where he often rode with Louis E. Stoddard, who was on the American team that played England in the twenties. Charles King, a wealthy broker, was born in 1873 into a prominent Chicago family of mortgage bankers. In 1894, when he left Yale, he joined the family firm of Shanklin and King, and in 1906 he organized his own firm—King, Farnum and Co. He kept two homes, in the winter living at 1450 Astor Street in Chicago, and in the summer on Ridge Road in Lake Forest. He later moved his business East, where he lived on Long Island. To Mr. King, Fitzgerald was from another world, and Fitzgerald became aware that he was considered socially beneath Ginevra. Most of this information came to me in an interview with Ginevra's sister, Mrs. Marjorie King Belden, who lived in Montecito, California. As Mrs. Belden bluntly told me, "My father often gave him [Fitzgerald] a piece of his mind." When I described Tom Buchanan to her, I asked if Tom had similarities to William Mitchell. Mrs. Belden consented that there were a number of similarities, but she went on to say that "I had described her father almost precisely."[22] There is no question that the experience with Ginevra King and her family left an indelible mark on Fitzgerald's psyche. If he had thought of himself as a poor boy in a rich man's world at Princeton, it was never to such a degree. But when he lost the girl he loved, he began to feel that his lack of money was the fault. Years later Fitzgerald was to advise his daughter to marry someone who follows a "calculated path stemming from a talent or money" (*Letters*, 71). He could say this and still distrust the very rich, seeing them in his sense of hurt as careless people.

The principal characters in *The Great Gatsby* thus begin to emerge: a great deal of Ginevra King went into Fitzgerald's conception of Daisy Fay; Tom Buchanan—who came from a wealthy Chicago family, went to Yale, owned a string of polo ponies on Long Island—is the fusion of Mr. King and William Mitchell; and Jordan Baker is Edith Cummings, a friend of Ginevra, just as Jordan is a friend of Daisy.

Fitzgerald came away from Ginevra with a sense of social inadequacy, a deep hurt, and longing for the girl beyond attainment. He expressed these sentiments first, not in *The Great Gatsby*, but in "Winter Dreams," published in *Metropolitan Magazine* in December 1922. In this story the two lovers are separated by money—Dexter Green is the son of a grocer, just as Fitzgerald's maternal grandfather was in the grocery business—and Judy Jones's father is as wealthy as his Pierce-Arrow automobile indicates. When he is twenty-three, Dexter falls in love with Judy, who encourages and then drops him. At twenty-five Dexter is engaged to another girl, but he breaks his engagement when Judy once again shows interest in him. When Judy has proved to herself her complete power over Dexter, she dismisses him once and for all from her life. At thirty-two, Dexter is a Jay Gatsby, preserving his "old" image of Judy, his "winter" dreams: Dexter learns at this time that Judy, who has since married, is having marital troubles and that she has "faded" and is considered "too old" for her husband. The news shocks him because suddenly he realizes that his youth is gone—and with it an ideal conception of perfect beauty that had kept the world resplendent and alive:

> He had thought that having nothing else to lose he was invulnerable at last—but he knew that he had just lost something more as surely as if he had married Judy Jones and seen her fade away before his eyes.
> The dream was gone. Something had been taken from him. . . .

For he had gone away and he could never go back any more. . . . Even the grief he could have borne was left behind in the country of illusion, of youth . . . where his winter dreams had flourished.

"Long ago," he said, "long ago, there was something in me, but now that thing is gone. . . . I cannot cry. I cannot care. That thing will come back no more." (*Stories*, 145)

As in "Winter Dreams," Fitzgerald gets these feelings of lost youth and beauty into *The Great Gatsby*. He also gets into the novel his sense of social inadequacy and his emotion of hurt when the dream is betrayed by lack of money. "The whole idea of Gatsby," Fitzgerald said, "is the unfairness of a poor young man not being able to marry a girl with money. This theme comes up again and again because I lived it."[23]

Fitzgerald had almost lost Zelda also because of his lack of money, but he finally won her. It was the wound over Ginevra that never healed (Fitzgerald described it "as the skin wound on a haemophile"). He kept all of Ginevra's letters to the end of his life. He even had them typed up and bound in a volume that runs to 227 pages.

The "dreams" in "Winter Dreams" are an eternal yearning for the promise of summer and the fulfillment of romance. When Fitzgerald lost Ginevra, he came to believe that such yearning was an end in itself; he believed in the need to preserve a romantic state of mind where the imagination and the will are arrested—in a state of suspension—by an idealized concept of beauty and love. The loss creates an eternal striving, and hope keeps the world beautifully alive.

When Gatsby kisses Daisy, his mind "would never romp again," his conception of beauty was fixed, and his will yearned eternally for that beauty. "It is sadder to find the past again," Fitzgerald once wrote, "and find it inadequate to the present than it is to have it elude you and remain forever a harmonious conception of memory."[24]

As long as one cares, the loss can keep the world alive with expectation. Nick Carraway expresses Gatsby's loss of expectation when he surmises that perhaps Gatsby "no longer cared" and, if so, then his sky must have suddenly become "unfamiliar," the leaves "frightening," and a rose "grotesque." As Daisy was the source of Gatsby's ideal beauty, Ginevra

Careless People: Daisy Fay

King was the source of Fitzgerald's. In October 1937, when he was writing for Hollywood, Fitzgerald went up to Santa Barbara to see Ginevra, who was there on a visit. He was overcome with fear because "She was the first girl I ever loved and I have faithfully avoided seeing her up to this moment to keep that illusion perfect" (*Letters*, 19).

Fitzgerald saw the need for a "perfect illusion" as part of the creative impulse. In "The Pierian Springs and the Last Straw," an early (1917) short story, the author gets his girl and then no longer feels the need to write. Not only did Ginevra King go into *The Great Gatsby*, she was in many ways part of Fitzgerald's motive for writing the novel in the first place. The romantic emotion the Fitzgerald hero experiences was inseparable from its object of attention. Once Daisy gave herself to Gatsby one resplendent October evening, she incarnates the dream (112). She embodies all the wonder and mystery that lies inherent in romantic possibility, so that to yearn for her is to romp like God through the heavens, to live life as sheer potentiality. So long as Gatsby does not have Daisy he can keep this godlike state of romantic yearning alive. Once he finally gains or loses her, the romantic possibility is gone forever, and Gatsby will sink to earth like the couch that seems to float down from the ceiling at the beginning of the novel; he will "never romp again like the mind of God" (112); the material world will once more lay claim to the unreal, and Gatsby will look up "at an unfamiliar sky through frightening leaves" to shiver at the grotesqueness of a rose and sunlight upon thin grass (162). The desire for Daisy energizes his world, fuels his very being; and when he loses her, romantic possibility is exhausted, a romantic state of mind depleted. The green grass loses its color, just as the green breast of the new world turns into the valley of ashes. It is at this point in the story that Gatsby is reclaimed by the living dead, by George Wilson, the agent of the valley of ashes as well as the agent of Gatsby's death.

That Daisy bears the burden of compelling such romantic intensity perhaps explains why she is presented so vaguely as a character. It is very hard to visualize her from the novel itself. When we first meet her, Nick spends more time describing her voice than her physical presence. What we learn about Daisy involves mostly her mannerisms. She speaks in a low, throaty voice, so that people must lean toward her when she speaks

(9). On some physical aspects of Daisy, Fitzgerald gives us conflicting information. At one point in the novel Daisy refers to her daughter's "yellowy hair," and then goes on to say, "She doesn't look like her father . . . She looks like me. She's got my hair and shape of the face" (117). And yet, when Gatsby and Daisy consummate their love one still October night, we are told that "he kissed her dark shining hair" (150).[25] Daisy can lack physical presence because it is more important that she embodies romantic expectation and lost time. Daisy's very name suggests something perishable as well as otherworldly. When Gatsby meets her five years after he lost her, the language of the novel gives way to plays and puns upon time. "Nobody's coming to tea," Gatsby says in panic, "It's too late!" (85). As Gatsby and Daisy meet, Gatsby knocks a clock from the mantelpiece, which he catches with trembling fingers (87). Once he again feels comfortable with Daisy, he begins to relax and to wind down like "an over-wound clock" (93).

Daisy is kept so vague and impalpable that Fitzgerald makes key mistakes in accounting for her chronology. We are told, for example, that Daisy and Gatsby fall in love in the summer and autumn of 1917 when Daisy is eighteen years old. The next autumn, 1918, she is described as "gay as ever"; she makes her debut "after the armistice," November 1918; is engaged to a man from New Orleans in February 1919; and in June 1919 she marries Tom Buchanan (76–77). Tom and Daisy honeymoon in the South Seas through June and July of 1919 and in August they are in Santa Barbara, where Tom gets in an accident on the Ventura highway with a chambermaid from the hotel (78). The next April, 1920, Daisy gives birth to her child. The novel, we know, takes place in the summer of 1922 and, we are told, the child is three years old. But if the child was born in April 1920, it would be two years and two months old, an error of fact that calls attention to itself in a novel so otherwise intricately weaved.

The physical facts controlling Daisy's existence ultimately give way to symbolic meaning, and she becomes more vague as the story becomes more dependent upon her fulfilling this function. Thus it is a bit unprofitable to argue about the moral meaning of Daisy. Some of the earlier critics of the novel were very hard on her. Marius Bewley refers to her "vicious emptiness"; Robert Ornstein calls her "criminally amoral"; and Alfred Kazin depicts her as "vulgar and inhuman." In the light of recent feminist criticism Daisy is seen as more victim than victimizer. Her life with Tom has not been an easy one; she has put up with his infidelities and his gibberish about racial and other matters. But a close reading of the text reveals that Daisy is also capable of her own gibberish, and that she has become more like Tom Buchanan than first impressions willingly admit. In a novel of careful narrative counterpointing, Fitzgerald depicts Daisy as both disingenuous and theatrical, even showing how Tom's mannerisms have become hers, before he juxtaposes Daisy's words, which are as silly as Tom's words, about the rise of the colored races. In recounting what she said when her daughter was born, Daisy tells Nick:

> "I woke up out of the ether with an utterly abandoned feeling, and asked the nurse right away if it was a boy or a girl. She told me it was a girl, and so I turned my head away and wept. 'All right,' I said, 'I'm glad it's a girl. And I hope she'll be a fool—that's the best thing a girl can be in this world, a beautiful little fool.'
>
> "You see I think everything's terrible anyhow," she went on in a convinced way. "Everybody thinks so—the most advanced people. And I *know*. I've been everywhere and seen everything and done everything." Her eyes flashed around her in a defiant way, *rather like Tom's,* and she laughed with thrilling scorn. "Sophisticated—God, I'm sophisticated!"
>
> The instant her voice broke off ceasing to compel my attention, my belief, I felt the basic insincerity of what she had said. It made me uneasy, as though the whole evening had been a trick of some sort to exact a contributory emotion from me. I waited, and sure enough, in a moment she looked at me with an absolute smirk on her lovely face, as if she had asserted her membership in a rather distinguished secret society to which she and Tom belonged. (17–18; second emphasis mine)

When Fitzgerald finally concretizes Daisy, it is always in terms of money. Her voice, Gatsby tells us, "is full of money" (120). And when Daisy returns to Gatsby after an absence of five years, Fitzgerald avoids giving us the substance of their response to each other by taking us on a tour of Gatsby's house, where Gatsby proves that he has earned enough money to deserve her love. Fitzgerald was so stung by his experience with the high rich that he could never break through his feelings of resentment against them, and Daisy becomes almost a caricature of that emotion. She is, to be sure, victimized by Tom, but she also embodies the world of which he is a part. In the denouement, the scene at the Plaza Hotel in chapter 7, Daisy simply becomes a kind of chess piece moved about in a game played by Tom and Gatsby, although it is totally to the point here that Tom triumphs over Gatsby by disclosing to Daisy the origins of Gatsby's money. The whole novel ultimately turns on what Daisy considers to be legitimate and illegitimate wealth, a blurred boundary given the fact that Walter Chase, Tom's friend, seems to be a bridge between the world of Tom and the world of Gatsby, and certainly an ironic point given the theme of the crooked broker.

Why Fitzgerald chose to model Gatsby on a crooked stockbroker is an interesting question. One answer is that perhaps this was Fitzgerald's private joke—a subtle way of getting back at Charles King and William Mitchell, both of whom were in the bond business. By modeling Gatsby on Edward Fuller, and then by allowing Gatsby to embody many of his own feelings, Fitzgerald was ironically depicting the gap between himself and the Kings-Mitchells. In this way, Jay Gatsby of West Egg becomes comically related to Tom Buchanan of East Egg; one is the ersatz parallel of the other.

In an apprentice story, "The Pierian Springs and the Last Straw" (*Nassau Literary Magazine,* October 1917), George Rombert has many of the qualities of *both* Jay Gatsby and Tom Buchanan. Like Gatsby, he loses the love of his life when he is betrayed by his "emotional imagination"; and when he loses his girl, time stops: "When I crossed the threshold," he says, "it was sixteen minutes after ten. At that minute I stopped living." Like Tom Buchanan, George Rombert is an overbearing bully. In *The Great Gatsby* Daisy accuses Tom of bruising her finger, and in this early story George Rombert breaks Myra's finger. The narrator, in another parallel to *The Great Gatsby,* has the same reservations about George Rombert that Nick Carraway has about Tom Buchanan, and he is not afraid to pass moral judgment: "My Uncle's [George Rombert's] personality had dropped off him like a cloak. He was not the romantic figure of the grill, but a less sure, less attractive and somewhat contemptible individual."²⁶ Myra's husband, we are told, is a broker—a "crooked broker," according to George Rombert, a "damn thief that robbed me of everything in this hellish world" (*Apprentice Fiction,* 172–73). In "The Pierian Springs and the Last Straw" we have the germ of Jay Gatsby and Tom Buchanan—and the theme of the "crooked broker." Fitzgerald later gave Tom and Gatsby separate qualities, modeling Gatsby on Edward Fuller and Tom on William Mitchell-Charles King. His models, however, were all brokers; and in *The Great Gatsby* there is an amusing, although slightly hidden, relationship between Gatsby and Tom Buchanan—both were, at least in conception, "crooked brokers." The broker will steal the object of love in Fitzgerald's late as well as early fiction. Tommy Barban, who takes Nicole Warren away from Dick Diver in *Tender Is the Night,* is, among other things, a broker.

Fitzgerald also saw that Edward Fuller's social position was a kind of grotesque embodiment of his own. He was rejected by Ginevra for being socially inferior. Fitzgerald extended the difference between himself and Ginevra by making Gatsby into the essence of the social impostor. At one point in *The Great Gatsby,* when Daisy seems about ready to leave Tom for Gatsby, they hear—ironically enough—the chords of Mendelssohn's "Wedding March" from the ballroom of the Plaza Hotel. Daisy suddenly remembers a man named Biloxi, who fainted at their wedding, and they discover that each thought that the other knew him. Biloxi, in fact, told Daisy that he was president of Tom's class at Yale. Biloxi, the impostor, embodies the very spirit of Gatsby in the world of Tom Buchanan. Tom, in fact, asks Gatsby if he went to Oxford "about the time Biloxi went to New Haven" (129). Biloxi, like Gatsby, is an exaggerated expression of Fitzgerald's own insecurity involving the high rich of Lake Forest and elsewhere.

Fitzgerald was doing something in *The Great Gatsby* that he had not done before. He was pushing his sense of experience away from the middle ground of verisimilitude toward extremes—toward two kinds of distortions. The dreamer distorted becomes Gatsby, a man whose hopelessly vulgar taste allows an eternal yearning for a meretricious beauty. The rich man distorted becomes Tom Buchanan, a man whose ruthlessness preserves his worldly comfort and whose shoddy ideas keep intact his sense of superiority. Both Gatsby and Tom Buchanan are men without conscience. Gatsby is just as intent on taking Daisy from Tom as Tom is on keeping Daisy from Gatsby. Both caricature Fitzgerald's own experience—his own sense of combat: the dreamer in conflict with a rigid reality; the promises of youth in conflict with the ravages of time; and the man of suspect means in conflict with the established rich. Fitzgerald let his sense of awe carry much of the meaning connected with Daisy as a character. That she is more symbolic than real perhaps explains why we have so many unanswered questions about her motives.

Fitzgerald himself was aware of these limitations. In a letter to Edmund Wilson shortly after publication of the novel, he admitted that he never was able to come to terms with "the emotional relations between Gatsby and Daisy from the time of their reunion to the catastrophe" (*Letters*, 341). Most absent from what we need to know about Daisy is what she told Tom in their kitchen over a plate of cold fried chicken and two bottles of ale after she had run over Myrtle Wilson. What transpires here Nick has no way of knowing. As he looks through the kitchen window, he sees a scene both intimate and intense. "They weren't happy, and neither of them had touched the chicken or the ale— and yet they weren't unhappy either. There was an unmistakable air of natural intimacy about the picture, and anybody would have said that they were conspiring together" (146). This is all that we know about this key scene—one of the most important scenes in the novel. The word "conspiring" suggests that Daisy does confide in Tom—and so the meaning of *The Great Gatsby* in some ways turns on one word. The narrative implications here are gigantic: if Tom knows that Daisy was driving Gatsby's car when he sends Wilson to Gatsby's house, then Tom kills Gatsby as clearly as if he pulled the trigger himself. If he does not know, then Daisy is equally complicit in Gatsby's death. Nick's anger at Tom at the end of the novel suggests that he believes Daisy told Tom the whole story and that both Tom and Daisy must share responsibility for Gatsby's death: "They were careless people," Nick tells us, "they smashed up things and creatures and then retreated back into their money or their vast carelessness, or whatever it was that kept them together, and let other people clean up the mess they had made. . . ." (180–81). Such moral disgust seems to have grounded Fitzgerald's own sense of pain and hurt when it came to the "careless rich." He had also bled on their sacrificial altar, as do Myrtle and George Wilson, and Gatsby. Tom and Daisy live off the energy of other people; they are the ultimate source of romantic depletion. What keeps their life splendid exhausts in a sacrificial way the lives of others; they turn the green world into dust. Myrtle Wilson literally "mingled her thick dark blood with the dust" they leave behind; and when Wilson kills Gatsby and then himself, Nick tells us, "the holocaust was complete" (163). The modern use of the word *holocaust* confuses the more precise meaning Fitzgerald brought to it. Behind the original meaning of the word is the idea of a sacrificial offering (which makes the word inappropriate when applied to Hitler's murdering of six million Jews). Gatsby, Myrtle, and George all die as sacrificial victims so that the Buchanan way of life can go on, their sense of superiority can be sustained, and their arrogance can remain inviolate. The Buchanans' wealth leaves behind the valley of ashes; their carelessness, victims. Daisy embodies the swing from the resplendence that makes up their world to the ugliness off of which such resplendence feeds. Tom Buchanan can afford to buy a $350,000 string of pearls for Daisy. Tom is next in line in the list that includes Dan Cody, James J. Hill, and Meyer Wolfsheim, men who moved across America amassing a fortune by removing the Indians and depleting the land, before returning to the modern city with its new institutions, controlled by the Tom Buchanans at one level and the Meyer Wolfsheims on another, who process all forms of money, exploited and otherwise. Behind this is the urge for power. In front is the resplendent world such power can buy and the women, like Daisy Fay, who incarnate its glamour and whose beauty is inseparable from the acts of such possession. At some point in his life Jay Gatsby bought into this dream and saw it as the purest form of romantic attainment. In *The Great Gatsby* Fitzgerald brilliantly saw the terrible price that went with the exhaustion of such romantic possibility.

9

"Civilization's Going to Pieces": Tom Buchanan

"Civilization's going to pieces," broke out Tom violently. "I've gotten to be a terrible pessimist about things. Have you read 'The Rise of the Colored Empires' by this man Goddard?" (13)

The idea of power in *The Great Gatsby* is embodied in Tom Buchanan. He is not only a man of powerful build and commanding presence, but he exudes a kind of authority as he ushers people about as well as forcing moral pronouncements upon them. He was also, for Fitzgerald, the embodiment of the high rich, a personality type that he investigated at length in his noteworthy story "The Rich Boy" (1926). In that story Anson Hunter (modeled in part on Ludlow Fowler, a classmate of Fitzgerald's at Princeton) is used to having his way, especially with women. When Paula Legendre refuses to submit to his emotional authority, he finds himself compelled to break her will; when that fails, he finds himself, ironically, in her power—a situation that drives him obsessively toward reversing the terms of their relationship. Tom Buchanan is not so obsessed, perhaps because his authority has seldom been challenged. When he finds himself on the verge of losing both his wife and his mistress, he becomes panicky, but the situation proves to be one that he can manage.

Behind Tom Buchanan are the dynamics of power, both personal and historical. These dynamics link Tom strangely with Dan Cody and James J. Hill, men who are the American equivalent of Robinson Crusoe.

"Civilization's Going to Pieces": Tom Buchanan

They come to the wilderness with a set of old myths and a semi-empirical state of mind, impose their will upon the land, and turn that control into wealth. The ending of Defoe's famous novel shows Robinson Crusoe dividing up the land so that he can sell it as real estate.

While Fitzgerald is hardly as explicit about this process as Defoe, all of these key elements inhere in *The Great Gatsby*. Historically, Tom is simply the last link in the chain that takes us from the explorers who first came to the new world (which Nick acknowledges at the end), to the Crusoe-like frontiersmen (Dan Cody/James J. Hill), who move west across the land until they reach the sea and then turn east toward the city, which is now both instrument to this new process of creating wealth and monument to its worldly success.

The city's presence in *The Great Gatsby* takes on immense importance because it marks the last link in a historical process that takes us from feudalism to modernism. We move, that is, from a feudal society dominated by the idea of birthrights to an urban society where natural rights have been subsumed to the privileges and advantages of wealth. We have moved, to put this differently, from Crusoe to Benjamin Franklin-Thomas Jefferson, to Daniel Boone-James J. Hill-Buffalo Bill Cody, to John D. Rockefeller-Jay Gould. We have moved from a world of peasantry to the bourgeoisie, from explorers to pioneers, from feudal faith to Enlightenment optimism, from landed aristocracy to robber baron, from frontier village to modern megalopolis—from one power structure to another, in the last of which Tom Buchanan is the titular head. The novel says all of this both directly and indirectly with narrative reference to Franklin, Boone, Cody, and Rockefeller, as well as reference to the pastoral origins of the city and the fact that the original owner of Gatsby's mansion cannot get the townspeople to thatch their roofs and behave like peasants (89). The architecture of the principal houses in the novel sustains this sense of the historical sweep, as we move from Gatsby's imitation Norman edifice, to Tom's Georgian mansion, to the middle-class apartment in urban New York that Tom uses for trysting purposes. This middle-class realm near the Bronx is inseparably connected with the depleted Main Street that runs through the Valley of Ashes and that takes Tom from one of his worlds to the other. That Gatsby modeled himself on Benjamin Franklin (174) and Dan Cody, and that his fate was connected to James J. Hill are allusions too pointed to miss.

Thus when we think of Tom Buchanan as a power broker in this novel, we must realize that the system of power he manipulates is one that has come at the end of a long line of varying power systems. There are a number of characteristics about Tom that on the surface remain puzzling. Since he is a foil to Gatsby, it is not surprising that he is depicted as an unsympathetic character. But why did Fitzgerald locate what is most objectionable about Tom in a context of race, scientific pronouncements, and a sense of exploitation? One might think of these matters as simply arbitrary qualities Fitzgerald imagined. But a look into the cultural moment in which Fitzgerald located the novel leads to a very different conclusion, and explains at the same time Fitzgerald's special attention to Oswald Spengler. Near the end of his life Fitzgerald wrote Maxwell Perkins that "I read [Spengler] the summer that I was writing *The Great Gatsby,* and I don't think I ever quite recovered from him" (*Letters,* 289-90). In 1927 Fitzgerald gave a long interview on his interest in Spengler, and critics have been conscious of the influence of Spengler on *Tender Is the Night* and a series of short stories about the Dark Ages that Fitzgerald wrote in the thirties.[27]

But the connection between Spengler and *The Great Gatsby* has seemed more tenuous because Spengler's *The Decline of the West,* originally published in 1918 (vol. 1) and 1922 (vol. 2), was not translated into English until 1926, and Fitzgerald could not read German. But this explanation is itself subject to important qualifications. First, the summer that Fitzgerald was writing *The Great Gatsby* he was living in Europe where Spengler's ideas had caused a sensation and were being discussed in ways that made them generally accessible. Second, at least nine articles or review-essays in English on Spengler and *The Decline of the West* were published between 1922 and the summer of 1924. One of the most detailed is an eight-thousand-word essay by W. K. Stewart, entitled "The Decline of Western Culture: Oswald Spengler's *Downfall of Western Civilization* Explained." This article appeared in the *Century* magazine in the summer of 1924, exactly the time that Fitzgerald tells Perkins that he was reading Spengler. Fitzgerald often read the *Century* (in *Tender Is the Night* Dick

Diver even buys it at a station quay, among other reading material, when he leaves for a trip). That this and other essays[28] made Spengler's basic ideas available to English readers is a fact that cannot be denied or dismissed. But to limit the discussion in this way is a disservice both to Fitzgerald and the history of ideas, which have a life larger than their source of publication. The Spenglerian conception of history is so descriptive of *The Great Gatsby* that one has to be literal-minded to the point of perversity in resisting the affinities of mind at work.

In *The Decline of the West* Spengler discussed three cultures that have experienced the process of growth and decay: the classical or Apollonian, the Mediterranean–Middle East or the Magian, and the medieval or the Faustian which is being replaced by the era of the newer modern Caesars. Each of these cultures is independent of the other; their destiny is inborn; the similarity of their history reveals a common process at work and not a causal connection between and among them. "Each culture has its own new possibilities of self-expression which arise, ripen, decay and never return."[29]

Spengler's theory of history comes directly from German romantic beliefs in the organic nature of society with a rejection of causal and mechanical connections. Each culture had a biological basis with a pattern of growth and decline parallel to that of human beings. For Spengler, the process of maturity gives way to decline when culture gives way to civilization—that is, when we move from a landed to an urban society, which he saw as a natural process giving way to an artificial process. Such polarities as destiny and causality, countryside and city, are at the very heart of Spengler's theory. As man moves away from the natural rhythms of the land, his sense of instinct is replaced by reason, his sense of nature and myth by scientific theory, and his sense of natural marketplace (barter and exchange) by abstract theories of money. As Spengler put it:

> Intelligence is the replacement of unconscious living by exercise in thought, masterly, but bloodless and jejune.... Hence ... the substitution of scientific theory, the causal myth, for the religious. Hence, too, money-in-the abstract as the pure causality of economic life, in

contrast to rustic barter, which is pulsation and not a system of tensions." (Spengler, 2:103)

Spengler ends this discussion by talking about "the sterility of civilized man."

Most relevant to *The Great Gatsby* is the idea of Faustian man. According to Spengler, Faustian man finds himself longing for the unattainable; has no sense of his limits; his imagination soars like his Gothic cathedrals to encompass the idea of infinity; his painting makes use of distant perspective, his music the expansive form of the fugue; his adventurers are long-distance sailors and explorers; and his modern heirs try to conquer space or create vast empires in the tradition of Cecil Rhodes, for whom "expansion is everything." While Faustian man lingers into the modern, he is transformed by the Enlightenment, which brings with it a sense of the empirical (in which reason is limited to the range of the senses and to the data the senses can collect) and the need for quantitative measurement. Under such influence, the sense of the infinite gives way to cold reason, science, and technology. Man, no longer at one with the land, moves to the city, which has become a money center. The rise of a new breed of money brokers turns the old world upside down. Spengler believed the movement from country to city involved a destructive process. In historical terms, culture gave way to civilization; in human terms, Faustian man gives way to Enlightenment man—the priest-king is replaced by the new Caesar, the man of money and power. When this happens a primitive sense of race is lost, and the decay embodied in the idea of civilization begins.

It takes no forcing whatever to see how Gatsby and Tom Buchanan play into these Spenglerian ideas: the story of Gatsby *is* the story of Faustian man, while Tom Buchanan embodies the rise of the new-moneyed Caesar who has come to power after Enlightenment science has transformed the mind. As Spengler put it, "Race, Time, and Destiny belong together. But the moment scientific thought approaches them, the word 'Time' acquires the significance of a dimension, the word 'Destiny' that of causal connection, while 'Race' . . . becomes an incomprehensible chaos of unconnected and heterogeneous characters" (Spengler, 2:130–31).

This passage explains much that otherwise appears accidental and gratuitous in Tom's character. What is important to see is that Tom has need for "scientific" explanations of his world. He tells us, "I read somewhere that the sun's getting hotter every year. . . . It seems that pretty soon the earth's going to fall into the sun—or wait a minute—it's just the opposite—the sun's getting colder every year" (118). That Tom's remarks are abstract, unfeeling, garbled, and contradictory is to the point, and reveals a quality of mind in keeping with Spengler's description of modern man who has been separated from the rhythms of nature by scientific systems of thought.

And not only is Tom unable to relate directly to the world of nature, he is also unable to relate directly to others outside his class and race. Near the beginning of the novel Tom expounds his racial theories which he has abstracted from a book: "The idea is if we don't look out the white race will be—will be utterly submerged. It's all scientific stuff; it's been proved. . . . It's up to us, who are the dominant race, to watch out or these other races will have control of things" (13). Spengler never offered such an offensive theory of race, but the idea of race was deeply embedded in his theory of Culture vs. Civilization. Spengler believed that "a race has roots. Race and landscape belong together." "A race," he continued, "does not migrate. Men migrate, and their successive generations are born in ever-changing landscapes" (Spengler, 2:119). But this is not a static process. When the landscape absorbs the new race, the culture remains; but when what is homogeneous and organic to the culture breaks down, civilization takes over. One can see as a backdrop in *The Great Gatsby* the Spenglerian transition taking place between culture and civilization in America. As Nick (Scottish-American) and Gatsby (German-American) motor into New York they enter a multiethnic world. On their way to meet Meyer Wolfsheim (an American Jew), they see a limousine with three blacks being driven by a white chauffeur, and a hearse filled with mourners "with the tragic eyes and short upper lips of southeastern Europe" (69). For over one hundred years immigrants and blacks were flocking into the eastern cities, one group from northern then eastern

Europe, the other from the American South. New York was the very embodiment of the process, a community now so heterogeneous that it would test to the limit Spengler's belief that the "secret force" of landscape could reunify such diversity:

> In place of a world there is a *city, a point,* in which the whole life of broad regions is collecting while the rest dries up. In place of a type-
> • true people, born of and grown on the soil, there is a new sort of nomad, cohering unstably in fluid masses, the parasitical city dweller, traditionless, utterly matter-of-fact, religionless. . . . (Spengler, 1:32)

While Spengler's observations are certainly relevant to matters of race in *The Great Gatsby,* Fitzgerald was probably more influenced in his thinking by Shane Leslie, a close friend of Father Sigourney Fay, his mentor at Newman Academy. In a review for the *Nassau Lit* and a letter to his cousin, Mrs. Richard Taylor, Fitzgerald had praised Leslie's books, especially *The Celt and the World* published by Scribner's in 1917. Leslie's theory of civilization was also primarily social (but not bigotedly so). He argued that from Aryan origins came two racial stocks—Teutons and Celts. The Celts were absorbed by Roman conquest or driven to remote parts of Europe (Ireland, Wales, Scotland, Cornwall, and Brittany). The Teutons came into power with the collapse of Rome, eventually rose to control Europe, especially England and Germany, where their Anglo-Saxon stock prevailed. Fitzgerald was drawn to Leslie's theory because it gave a twilight-glory quality to Celticism (the source of his own origins) that appealed to his seemingly natural instinct for a cultural pessimism.

What Leslie had worked out as a kind of bittersweet explanation of Celtic history became an insidious form of racism in the hands of Lothrop Stoddard. His book, *The Rising Tide of Color,* also published by Scribner's in 1920, is the work that Tom Buchanan is referring to when he asks Nick if he has read "'The Rise of the Colored Empires' by this man Goddard?" (13). Stoddard divided the white race into three groups: Nordics, Alpine, and Mediterranean. He believed those who did not remain in the Mediterranean region had migrated north into places like Ireland. The Alpine people were the peasants of Europe who moved west into Spain and Portugal and east into the Slavic states. During the French Revolution, Stoddard maintained, the Alpine people came into power. But the great masters of Europe, he proclaimed, were the Nordics. They came south, conquered Rome, and built and controlled Europe up to World War I. While Stoddard never mentions Shane Leslie by name, in another book, *Racial Realities in Europe,* he refers to the Leslie thesis:

> An English writer once called his country Teutonic with a Celtic fringe. Translating this into modern racial terms [that is, into Stoddard's own racial terms], we can say that the population of Britain is predominantly Nordic, with a Mediterranean element that varies widely in different parts of the island.[30]

Given the racial encoding that is inherent in Stoddard's definition of Alpine and Mediterranean stock, one can easily see why Fitzgerald would be offended by the way Stoddard turned Leslie's book against itself, making it a shamelessly racist attack on all who are not Nordics.[31]

And it *is* offensive the way Stoddard bewails the loss of Nordic superiority in his books: "In the United States especially," Stoddard maintained, "recent immigration has brought in floods of Alpine and Mediterranean blood, and unless immigration from Southern and Eastern Europe is restricted and kept restricted the racial character of the American people will be rapidly and radically altered" (Stoddard, 19). Stoddard goes on to describe the racial mix one finds on a New York subway in contrast to the greater sense of racial homogeneity in a London tube (Stoddard, 36). Stoddard's belief in Nordic superiority is the basis for Tom's pronouncement that "We're Nordics. . . . And we've produced all the things that go to make civilization—oh, science and art, and all that. Do you see?" (14).

Fitzgerald superimposed Stoddard's theory of race upon Spengler's theory of civilization and used it as a means to both contextualize and characterize Tom Buchanan. As the new, moneyed Caesar, Tom in Spengler's historical paradigm not only replaces the Faustian Gatsby but is subject to the threat of the "rising tide of color" because Spengler believed that, as in Rome, the Caesars would eventually be overcome by conquerors analogous to the barbarians. These conquerors Spengler connected with what today we would call the Third World, emerging people who are beginning to employ modern technology that they will eventually use against the Western world. At one point in the novel Fitzgerald described Tom as if "he saw himself standing alone on the last barrier of civilization" (130). Tom's racism is thus consistent with his dominant but vulnerable position in the Spenglerian scheme of history as well as with his deprived moral values.

Tom takes great pride in modern science and progress, can never understand the state of mind that this kind of mentality has replaced, is scornful of the distant past, and cancels all other cultures in the name of Nordic superiority. When Enlightenment man, according to Spengler, substituted empirical for intuitive reasoning, the Faustian sense of mystery gave way to modern science—and to technology and the machine, which takes us to another key theme in *The Great Gatsby*. Repeatedly the characters talk about the automobile and careless driving until it becomes a major refrain. The owl-eyed man is in the car that wrecks its wheel leaving Gatsby's party; Tom is involved with another woman in a car shortly after his honeymoon (his infidelities obviously began early); Jordan Baker (whose name is taken from the names of two cars) drives recklessly; and, of course, Daisy runs over Myrtle in Gatsby's chrome-swollen car. Spengler actually concluded his discussion of the fate of the West with a chapter entitled "The Machine," which points out that the rise of the machine is accompanied by the demise of Faustian man. Man reversed his relationship with nature in that period of time from the rise of book printing to the invention of the steam engine, "which upset everything and transformed economic life from the foundations up. Till then nature rendered services, but now she was tied to the yoke *as a slave. . . .* And these machines become in their forms less and ever less human" (Spengler, 2:502–3). The machine separated man from nature, transformed the landscape, helped create the modern city, and enlarged the scale on which man lived as life became "less and ever less human." In a phrase, the machine created the world of Tom Buchanan.

This world was now totally urban, to refer again to Spengler. "In place of a world, there is a *city, a point,* in which the whole life of broad regions is collecting while the rest dries up." Once this happens, Spengler continued, the power system becomes inseparable from money: "the money-spirit . . . penetrates unremarked the historical forms of the people's existence" (I: 32–33). Spengler's words are in themselves a commentary on the text. Tom is a broker; Nick has come to New York to study the brokerage business by working in a brokerage firm. While waiting for Daisy to appear at their fateful reunion, Gatsby reads from a book on economics, an appropriate way to spend time waiting for a woman whose voice is full of money. Many *Gatsby* readers never realize how deeply Gatsby is connected with the underworld bond and brokerage business. When Gatsby asks Nick to arrange the meeting with Daisy, he tells him that he is in the bond business (83). When Tom confronts Gatsby at the Plaza Hotel, he insinuates that Gatsby's business is more than just bootlegging. "'That drug-store business was just small change,' continued Tom slowly, 'but you've got something on now that Walter's afraid to tell me about'" (135). And when Nick answers the phone, after Gatsby's death, the unsuspecting caller tells him that one of Gatsby's bondmen has been arrested (167).

Money, legally and illegally obtained, dominates the text, and ultimately carries the final authority of textual meaning. To that extent Tom becomes a central presence in the novel, an arbiter of final value, as in a totally different way Squire Allworthy, Mr. Knightley, and Esther Summerson become the final sources of reference in novels by Fielding, Austen, and Dickens. When Nick reveals the name of the firm for which he works, Tom dismisses it out of hand: "'Never heard of them,' he remarked decisively" (10). And it is, of course, Tom who turns the novel around by merely telling Daisy the origins of Gatsby's money (133–34).

It is interesting that when Gatsby's illegal activities are revealed, Jordan Baker reverts to her old snobbish self. Jordan is, of course, the feminine equivalent of Tom with her slim, masculine build, her authority in sports, and her willingness to refer most matters to materialistic value. That Jordan, Tom, and Daisy are the most careless of drivers links them literally with the machine and, by extension, with what the machine has come to symbolize in Spenglerian terms. It is thus appropriate that the final act of the novel turns on Tom's telling George Wilson that Gatsby owned the car that ran over Myrtle; not only does the agent of the valley of ashes become the agent of Gatsby's death, but the modern, moneyed Caesar is instrumental in the death of the last of the Faustian men. One does not have to read Spengler to understand *The Great Gatsby*, but once Spengler is overlaid upon the narrative, the text takes on a much deeper, historically resonant meaning.

10

Sugar Lumps and Ash Heaps:
George and Myrtle Wilson

Over the great bridge . . . with the city rising up across the river in white heaps and sugar lumps all built with a wish out of nonolfactory money. The city seen from the Queensboro Bridge is always the city seen for the first time, in its first wild promise of all the mystery and the beauty in the world.

A dead man passed in a hearse heaped with blooms. . . . (69)

This is a valley of ashes—a fantastic farm where ashes grow like wheat into ridges and hills and grotesque gardens. (23)

Three settings dominate *The Great Gatsby,* and they descend metaphorically from the resplendent Georgian mansion of Tom Buchanan at East Egg to the luxurious but déclassé Normandy castle of Gatsby among the arrivistes of West Egg to the valley of ashes through which one has to pass in order to reach the city where one can find the high rich in the Plaza Hotel, the Wolfsheims and Buchanans at lunch in their Manhattan coves, and the apartment at 158th Street that Tom keeps for his lovemaking with Myrtle Wilson. Each of these settings takes on a symbolic meaning of its own, ending with the hell of the middle class, figured in the men with spades who work on the top of the ash mounds. Tom's mansion embodies the taste that established money knows how to buy. Impressive in its gaudy way, Gatsby's house is to Nick more like a world's fair, a place where the rules of conduct are more appropriate to an amusement park than a sedate residence of the established rich.

As Nick's taxi takes him home one night, he thinks his house is on fire, so bright is the evening sky. But what he is seeing are the lights from

Gatsby's lawn. "Your place looks like the World's Fair," Nick tells Gatsby. "Does it?" Gatsby responds, and then follows with what seems to be a non sequitur: "Let's go to Coney Island, old sport. In my car" (82). Gatsby is happy to turn his house into a kind of Coney Island, a realm of respite from the toil of the city to which the urban restless can turn for release, until Daisy frowns on its inherent sleaziness. She was "offended" by it, Nick tells us, "appalled by West Egg, this unprecedented 'place' that Broadway had begotten upon a Long Island fishing village— appalled by its raw vigor that chafed under the old euphemisms and by the too obtrusive fate that herded its inhabitants along a short-cut from nothing to nothing. She saw something awful in the very simplicity she failed to understand" (108).

West Egg is to New York what Las Vegas is now to Los Angeles or Atlantic City to Philadelphia—a place to drift without purpose, to fill what would otherwise be empty time. No matter how superficially or crassly filled, time is the one thing in this novel that everyone tries not to empty. "What'll we do with ourselves this afternoon?" Daisy asks, "and the day after that, and the next thirty years?" (118). The rush away from such emptiness takes the principal characters into the city, that symbol of expectation, of rife excitement, and of undisclosed meaning. That is why the city can be described as something about to unfold with "wild promise" and "all the mystery and the beauty in the world" (69). As soon as Nick makes this pronouncement about the city, he sees a hearse carrying a dead man, and the novel quickly empties his sense of romantic possibility. The physical embodiment of this emptiness is the valley of ashes and its urban counterpart, the small apartment on 158th Street where Tom takes Myrtle. This building itself is a "slice in a long white cake of apartment houses" (28), the metaphor sustaining the sugar-lump imagery Fitzgerald also connects with the city.

The apartment itself is a caricature of upper-class taste. The living room is "crowded to the doors with a set of tapestried furniture entirely too large for it" (29). The tapestry involves ladies swinging in the gardens of Versailles. On the walls is a "portrait" by Chester McKee, the photographer who lives downstairs, whose photographs become an absurd middle-class attempt to approximate genuine art. We are told that he has 127

Sugar Lumps and Ash Heaps: George and Myrtle Wilson

photographs of Mrs. McKee, as if his work were equivalent to the catalog of a great artist. His landscape photos are described as "studies"— such as *Montauk Point—the Gulls* and *Montauk Point—the Sea.* Someone suggests that he do Myrtle's "portrait," and there is a discussion about the aesthetics of lighting; then Tom suggests that McKee do a study of George Wilson, Myrtle's husband—"*George B. Wilson at the Gasoline Pump,* or something like that" (32–33).

Myrtle tries desperately to maintain a facade of wealth and respectability; she believes that she is playing the role of the great matron: "'I told that boy about the ice.' Myrtle raised her eyebrows in despair over the shiftlessness of the lower orders. 'These people! You have to keep after them all the time.'" Myrtle then sweeps into the kitchen as if "a dozen chefs awaited her orders there" (32). This is a world of pretense, held together by vain hopes and a sense of self-worth that depends mainly upon a bigotry that can reduce others to a realm of inferiority. When this world is emptied of its crass hope and pretense, we have the valley of ashes—the dumping ground of emptied romantic expectation, even the gaudy expectations of a Myrtle Wilson.

Appropriately, then, the principal residents of the valley of ashes are George and Myrtle Wilson. They are really two sides of the same social coin: Myrtle still has "vitality about her as if the nerves of her body were continually smouldering" (25), an image that is appropriate to her place in the valley of ashes. George, on the other hand, is already beaten down by life, has long since lost anything like vitality, and is described by Nick as an "anaemic" and "spiritless man" whom people walk around "as if he were a ghost" (25). And ghost he is, similar to the walking dead that populate T. S. Eliot's *The Waste Land,* which Fitzgerald knew by heart.

A number of critics have connected *The Great Gatsby* and *The Waste Land.* The similarities cry out for attention. Like *The Waste Land, Gatsby* moves between and among people of different classes, like the upper class neurasthenic lady in her boudoir, the women discussing marriage and abortion in the pub, and the woman in her flat awaiting the sexual visit of the young man carbuncular. *The Waste Land* is also set against an urban background. At the beginning of the poem we see the walking dead enter King William Street, the Wall Street of London, ironically called to their secular chores by the bells of St. Mary Woolnoth. In an earlier version of the poem Eliot described a sea-journey to the North Pole in search of pelts and other wealth. This search for profit becomes a death-journey, a symbol of the destructive nature of rapaciousness and greed. Such greed has absorbed the last of religious instincts. St. Augustine goes unheeded in the secular city; Christ is unrecognized by his disciples on the road from Emmaus.

Fitzgerald was certainly influenced by *The Waste Land*. He sent Eliot a copy of his just-published novel, and Eliot responded with the now famous pronouncement that *The Great Gatsby* was the first advance in the novel since Henry James. One can see the basis for this mutual admiration. But even more important than thematic similarity is the fact that the two works function technically in the same way. *The Great Gatsby* is a kind of prose-poem, held together by image and symbol in the same way that *The Waste Land* shores up broken images against their ruin. Fitzgerald's language resonates with passages from the poem. Nick talks about "in the early morning the sun threw my shadow westward as I hurried down the white chasms of lower New York to the Probity Trust" (56); he continues, "again at eight o'clock, when the dark lanes of the Forties were five deep with throbbing taxicabs" (57); and Daisy remarks, "what'll we do with ourselves this afternoon" (118). (Cf. Eliot's "Your shadow at morning striding behind you / Or your shadow at evening rising to meet you" [lines 28–29], "What shall we do tomorrow? What shall we ever do" [lines 133–34], "At the violet hour . . . when the human engine waits / Like a taxi throbbing waiting" [lines 215–17].)

Beyond this catalog of borrowing is a cultural statement each work is making in terms of the other. *The Waste Land* was Eliot's response to a postwar Europe experiencing radical change. Historically, one empire after another had fallen, the last being the Hapsburgs, with Great Britain in line to be the next "falling tower." Eliot depicts a world coming morally apart, a world that has no principle to hold it together. We see the rich with nerves on end; middle-class housewives caught entrapped in sterile and purposeless lives; and lower-class clerks seeking mere gratification, no matter how mechanical or unfulfilling.

All of these people are culturally empty. Like Henry Adams, Eliot believed that every society needed some kind of mythic meaning to give it center and direction; an obsession for profit was not enough. Man had lost his primitive energy, had lost the basis for the Fisher King whose sacrificial vitality had been handed down in the form of Osiris, Adonis, Atiz, Tamuz, to Christ. Their vitality was now being played out, exhausted, in the post-Enlightenment world of science and technology. Gatsby brings the intensity of this lost vision to life, complete with its religious nature, something we know from Fitzgerald's original conception of the novel and from our own analysis of its religious motifs. Such intensity takes on a romantic vitality that Gatsby incarnates in Dan Cody and Daisy Fay. At the moment when the *idea* of Dan Cody can no longer hold Gatsby's world together, Gatsby tells Nick "the strange story of his youth and Dan Cody—told it to me because 'Jay Gatsby' had broken up like glass against Tom's hard malice, and the long secret extravaganza was played out" (148). At the moment Gatsby is deprived of such intensity, his imaginative conception of self becomes exhausted and the world around him changes before his eyes: the resplendent gives way to "an unfamiliar sky" whose materiality brings a shiver.

This sense of the exhaustion of romantic possibility was inseparable from the postwar sense of world weariness that we find in both the story that Nick Carraway tells and in the story Tiresias tells in *The Waste Land*. Eliot in turn drew upon Hermann Hesse's *Blick ins Chaos*. But the work that perhaps most subsumes both Fitzgerald's and Eliot's statements is one that we have already discussed, Spengler's *Decline of the West*. The sense of both religious and romantic intensity that Eliot and Fitzgerald felt slipping away, Spengler saw embodied in Faustian man, whose spirit was also being exhausted: "Force, Will, has an aim," Spengler tells us, "and where there is an aim there is for the inquiring eye an end. . . . The Faust . . . is dying. . . . What the myth of Götterdämmerung signified of old, the irreligious form of it, the theory of Entropy, signifies today" (Spengler, 1:423–24). The change of terminology here is important: to move from the idea of romantic depletion (as suggested in metaphors of waste and ashes) to the idea of entropy moves the discussion from a religious/mythic context to the scientific one involving entropy. Entropy results when, in a closed system, molecules become uniform and lose their capacity to do work. The application of Newton's second law of thermo-dynamics remotely interested even Tom Buchanan in his discussions of whether the sun is heating up or cooling down (118).

Henry Adams, of course, substituted entropy for apocalypse in his assessment of the fate of modern man. And Thomas Pynchon picked up where Adams left off in *The Crying of Lot 49*, which is a postmodern version of the *Gatsby* story. In Pynchon's novel another American Crusoe has built an empire: Pierce Inverarity is far more a builder and shaker than Tom Buchanan. To untangle his legacy becomes the fate of Oedipa Maas, more a Nick Carraway than a Gatsby figure, who, like her namesake, must come to terms with the world of the metaphorical father (*The Great Gatsby* actually opens with the words of Nick's father). She must solve the riddle of the city (a realm that fascinates Nick, who also walks its streets as he desires to be both "within and without" its powers) and come to terms with the Trystero. In creating his empire, Pierce Inverarity has given rise to a wasteland world, embodied in the Trystero, whose origins are coincidental with the rise of capitalism. The Trystero have moved West as a counterforce to Enlightenment progress, across an ocean, then across a continent to San Narciso (the city as monument to self), where they incorporate the dereliction and waste that the system casts off. They incorporate, that is, George and Myrtle Wilson.

Narratively we have moved a long way from Fitzgerald to Pynchon, but the idea that controls *The Great Gatsby* is very similar to the idea that controls *Lot 49*. Both works find their origins in the romantic belief in an infinite potentiality of self that plays itself out in a mechanistic world of limits, where such ideals are exhausted by the malice of Tom Buchanan or lose themselves in the labyrinth of Pierce Inverarity's System. When he comes in search of Gatsby, George Wilson is so rarefied that he seems like the vapor of a dream, a disembodied ghost (162). George, whose dreams have long been depleted, is bullied by Tom Buchanan, who robs him of Myrtle, his last wellspring of vitality; Gatsby, whose dreams have just died, breaks like glass also against Tom's hard malice when Tom robs the dream of substance by reclaiming Daisy. When George, sent in murderous pursuit by Tom, fires the fatal shots into Gatsby, he kills a soulmate, an ideological brother, a cultural embodiment of his very self. With the death of the dream the romantic sky is transformed, to be seen "through frightening leaves." With the exhaustion of romantic possibility the valley of ashes claims the dreamer, something that Henry Adams, Oswald Spengler, Hermann Hesse, and T. S. Eliot knew before Fitzgerald, and that Thomas Pynchon would know after him. The death of the dream foreshadows the death of the dreamer. One of Fitzgerald's most brilliant ironies in *The Great Gatsby* was to have those characters who are most depleted of romantic expectation and promise become the subject and object of the novel's climactic victimization.

11

Careless Driving: Nick Carraway

"You said a bad driver was only safe until she met another bad driver?
Well, I met another bad driver, didn't I? I mean it was careless of me to
make such a wrong guess. I thought you were rather an honest,
straightforward person. I thought it was your secret pride."
"I'm thirty," I said, "I'm five years too old to lie to myself and call it
honor." (179)

In many ways Nick Carraway is the most complex character in *The Great
Gatsby*. His story is not as complex as Gatsby's but it comes to parallel
Gatsby's in interesting ways, and Nick does bring a consciousness to the
novel that Gatsby does not have. Nick functions as a grand mediator in
this novel. Not only does he mediate between the world of Gatsby and
the Buchanans, but also between the text and Fitzgerald's use of him as a
narrator. To this extent, Nick is a character in his own right, and he is a
spokesman for Fitzgerald. The two are not identical in function and purpose, a fact that can lead to critical misunderstandings of the text.

The history of Nick's family embodies the history of Western civilization. His ancestors, he claims, were aristocrats and he is descended
from the Dukes of Buccleuch. When the aristocracy was played out with
the end of feudalism, his family became respectable bourgeoisie. It was
his granduncle who came to America at that cataclysmic moment of the
Civil War, when the agrarian South was giving way to the industrial
North. Interestingly, his granduncle sent a substitute to fight the war for
him and started the wholesale hardware business in the West that brings
his family their money and that his father runs at the time Nick tells us
the story of Gatsby. Nick's family has thus moved from Europe to Amer-

ica, from a feudal-agrarian base to an industrial one, and in America from the East coast to the Midwest. That Nick himself becomes disillusioned with the East at the same time as he locates certain residual values in the West will, as we shall see, become one of the dominant themes of the novel—as well as a growing preoccupation of Fitzgerald himself.

The story Nick tells involves retrospective narration. At the beginning of the novel he tells us that one year has elapsed since the death of Gatsby (2), and at the end of the novel he tells us that two years have elapsed (164). The difference in time, we presume, is the time it took Nick to tell (write?) his story. As the critics have long pointed out, the function of Nick is that of Conrad's Marlow in stories like *Lord Jim* and *Heart of Darkness*. Like Marlow, Nick takes on meaning in his own right, and the telling of his story can never be totally separated from our own sense of him as a character. Nick tells us more than he seems to know, and he knows more than he fully understands. Since he is the only character in the novel who has an inner sense of reality, we know Nick in a way that we do not know Fitzgerald's other characters, and for this reason it is probably easier for critics to like or dislike him. On the one hand, we have critics who think of him almost totally as a snob, as dishonest beyond redemption, and as a kind of wimp who lets Tom Buchanan off the moral hook at the end of the novel. On the other hand, we have critics who believe that he is reliable, that he grows in moral awareness, and that he embodies the moral affirmation of the novel's ending.

It is unlikely that another critical discussion can resolve such firm disagreement, but perhaps it can put some of it in perspective. It is, I think, relevant to keep in mind what we know about Nick from himself and what we know about him from drawing our own judgments from his behavior and what we think of his words. That he is a snob is something he tells us himself on the first page of the novel. But in a novel that is so concerned with social hierarchy, it is not surprising that snobs exist. One can say for Nick in this context that his snobbery is vastly different from that of the Buchanans, whose money allows them to feel socially superior to the world around them. Nick does not have enough money to justify that kind of snobbery, but he does feel morally superior to those around him. Thus Nick from the very beginning feels superior to both Tom and

Daisy, but especially Tom, whose vast fortune feeds into a sense of power that allows him to use people like things for his own well-being. Whether he is dealing with George Wilson's wife or with the car that Wilson wants to buy makes no difference; he will do what suits him best. He believes that both the car and the woman are there for his use, to be disposed as best serves his own interest, something to be done without moral obligation or a sense of guilt. Nick has known Tom at Yale, so it is not surprising that he has this impressive insight into Tom's character when he first calls upon Tom and Daisy. Tom has not changed—only the situation. But even Nick is a bit surprised by how callously Tom treats Daisy, at the same time as Nick is quite unsympathetic to her for allowing it to happen. "I was confused and a little disgusted," Nick tells us as he leaves after dinner. "It seemed to me that the thing for Daisy to do was to rush out of the house, child in arms—but apparently there were no such intentions in her head" (20–21). Daisy, in other words, knows what she is getting when she stays with Tom; his infidelity is the price she pays for such security, a security that she also will retreat back into when she not only dismisses Gatsby from her life but allows him to die for a crime that she committed. This hard-minded sense of self-interest separates the Buchanans from Nick. It is thus ironic that Nick finds himself falling in love with Jordan Baker, whose own sense of self-interest and social superiority makes her morally inseparable from the Buchanans.

Nick is both attracted and repulsed when he first sees Jordan. He finds her haughty, supercilious manner offensive, at the same time that he is attracted to her slender, hard body and her "charming, discontented face," whose eyes stare back at him with a "reciprocal curiosity" (11). Nick finds himself growing more interested in Jordan as they begin to run into each other during the summer—first at Gatsby's party and then at a house party in Warwick, New York. It is at the house party that Nick discovers that Jordan can leave a convertible car in the rain with the top down and then lie about it, at which time he remembers that a charge had been made—and then dropped—that she had cheated at golf. Nick challenges Jordan directly with his own charges of moral carelessness, which he sees embodied in her careless driving. "You're a rotten driver," he tells her. "Either you ought to be more careful, or you oughtn't to drive at all"

(59). She can take satisfaction in the fact that she is safe until she meets another careless driver, a charge she will bring against Nick himself at the end of the novel (179). Thus Jordan's remark that she hates careless people, "That's why I like you" (59), seems totally ironic, as does Nick's own claim that he is one of the "few honest people" he has ever known (60). Nick's growing entanglement with Jordan not only parallels his telling of the Gatsby-Daisy story, it raises questions at the outset about his own moral integrity and veracity.

But despite these challenges to Nick as character, we never lose an affinity for him because his deceit seems more unintentional than calculated. Moreover, his willingness to encourage Jordan seems to coincide with his own vicarious involvement in the Gatsby-Daisy story; the more he becomes witness to the intensity of Gatsby's attraction toward Daisy, the more willing he is to encourage Jordan Baker. It can hardly be an accident of narration that Nick kisses Jordan for the first time and becomes more romantically involved with her after she tells him one summer afternoon over tea in the Plaza Hotel the story of how Daisy and Gatsby fell in love. Later that evening, as they ride through Central Park, Nick will put his arms around Jordan and, before he kisses her for the first time, will think, "There are only the pursued, the pursuing, the busy, and the tired" (81). The intensity of Gatsby's love for Daisy so moves Nick that he reduces all life to the level of intensity on which it is lived, to the energy that infuses romantic dreams before they are emptied of meaning, leaving the disappointed and the tired. Nick somehow thinks that he can escape this fate, that only lesser mortals—like George Wilson—are subject to such an ending. That this also is a self-lie will be another one of the truths that he will learn from the telling of Gatsby's story.

Nick's initial moment of awareness comes in the crucial scene at the Plaza Hotel when Tom discloses the source of Gatsby's money and ruins forever the possibility of Gatsby ever winning Daisy with his criminal money. Nick realizes that romantic expectation, no matter how intensely conceived, cannot function independently of social reality. As Nick witnesses Gatsby's undoing, he tells us that these events occurred on his birthday—that he was thirty. Thirty marks the end of youth, the end of youthful commitment, the reckless pursuit of the dream. At some point reality has to temper romantic expectation, achievement or its lack must be factored into the moral equation; no matter how bitter that truth may be, we must accept responsibility for what we are—or are not. Nick comes to this conclusion in two steps. First, he thinks of what the future holds for him: "Thirty—the promise of a decade of loneliness, a thinning list of single men to know, a thinning briefcase of enthusiasm, thinning hair" (136). But, he rationalizes, perhaps Jordan can save him from such an ordeal—Jordan, "who, unlike Daisy, was too wise ever to carry well-forgotten dreams from age to age." The hope he attaches to Jordan is inseparable from the hope that he connects with the city itself, inseparable from the "dark bridge" from which Nick saw the city, resplendent in its wild promise of mystery and beauty, as he drove into New York with Gatsby. But this city is also inseparable from death, symbolized by the black hearse that passes them on the bridge. It is thus appropriate that as Nick and Jordan drive back to West Egg, they pass "over the dark bridge," and Jordan's wan face on his shoulder seems, for a moment, to reassure him. But such reassurance is only momentary for, as the next line tells us, they drive on "toward death" in the cooling twilight (137). So once more, a sense of promise and the reality of death are juxtaposed in this novel.

And it is the death of Myrtle Wilson—with all the moral carelessness that Nick connects with her ending—that is the final turning point in his relationship with Jordan. Such a relationship, he learns, has consequences too serious to be belied. When Tom, Nick, and Jordan arrive at the Buchanan house, Nick refuses to go in, despite Jordan's imploring. "I'd be damned if I'd go in," he tells us, "I'd had enough of all of them for one day, and suddenly that included Jordan too. She must have seen something of this in my expression, for she turned abruptly away and ran up the porch steps into the house" (143). When Jordan calls him at the office the next day, he refuses to see her, in effect breaking with her for good. Just before he leaves the East, he sees Jordan for the last time, and she points out that he too was less than honest in his relationship with her, that he knew what she was and still encouraged her. "You said a bad driver was only safe until she met another bad driver? Well, I met another bad driver, didn't I? I mean it was careless of me to make such a wrong guess. I thought you were rather an honest, straightforward person. I thought it was your secret pride" (179). Jordan's charge has much to justify it, and Nick now knows it. "I'm thirty," he tells her, "I'm five years too old to lie to myself and call it honor" (179).

Nick learns that romantic intensity untempered by self-knowledge and social responsibility is a moral form of recklessness. Nick has seen the dangers of Gatsby's romantic intensity and tried to warn him of its consequences. Even the afternoon when Gatsby and Daisy were reunited, Nick intuits a kind of recklessness in the love that Gatsby brings to Daisy: "the colossal vitality of his illusion" had simply "gone beyond her, beyond everything" (97). Later, Nick tells Gatsby, "I wouldn't ask too much of her. . . . You can't repeat the past" (111). Unlike Gatsby, Nick is not trying to seal the hole in time, to recuperate the lost past, recover some idea of himself that had gone into loving a woman. Also unlike Gatsby, he learns a truth that will forever separate him from the world of the Buchanans: that the creation of self involves more than a dream; that pursuits of the heart involve risks and moral consequences; and that desire, no matter how intense, finds its limits in the physical world. There romantic intensity and physical reality can collide—just as cars collide or run over people throughout the novel. Romantic possibility demands physical limits, even as we dare to be what we are not. *The Great Gatsby* may be a novel without a moral frame of reference, but Nick is a character striving to supply, for himself and for us, a moral center. I say "striving" because ultimately the moral center—like so much that is seen in this novel—comes to us slightly blurred.

The Great Gatsby never answers two major narrative questions. The first is, did Tom know that Daisy was driving the car that had killed Myrtle Wilson? The second question involves the ending of the novel, specifically what Nick is trying to assert when he claims a kind of superiority of the West over the East and when he himself returns to the West of his childhood where we find him at the beginning of the novel.

In his correspondence with Maxwell Perkins, Fitzgerald indicated that he was not totally happy with chapters 6 and 7 of his novel. These were the chapters that followed the reunion of Gatsby and Daisy. Up to this point Gatsby had seemed too vague to Perkins, and there were too many unanswered questions about the origin of his money. Fitzgerald began to revise the novel, giving us more information about Gatsby as he went along. He moved much of the long history of Gatsby in chapter 8 to chapter 6, thus giving the reader more of Gatsby's background before the fateful confrontation between Gatsby and Tom in chapter 7. After the novel was published Fitzgerald still had some reservations about the effectiveness of these chapters. When the sales of the novel disappointed him, he felt that it was because of the weakness of these chapters. He wrote Edmund Wilson that the most serious weakness was his not knowing in more detail what Daisy's response would have been to a man like Gatsby. The vagueness here, although unrecognized by the reviewers, nevertheless, he felt, affected the reading of the text. It had gone unnoticed because, he maintained, he had covered it with a blanket of beautiful prose.

But it is strange that in all of this commentary on narrative lapses neither Fitzgerald nor Perkins nor the reviewers commented on the most interesting narrative lapse: whether Daisy told Tom that she was driving the car that killed Myrtle Wilson. The closest we come to an answer is the scene in which Nick walks to the back of the Buchanan house, looks through the kitchen window, and sees Tom and Daisy talking over an untouched plate of cold chicken and untouched bottles of ale. The scene had an "air of natural intimacy" about it, Nick tells us, "and anybody would have said that they were conspiring together" (146). The key word is, of course, "conspiring"; it does suggest collusion, Tom sharing in Daisy's knowing that she was responsible for Myrtle's death. If that is the case, Fitzgerald certainly makes much turn on this single word, and many readers may find the meaning of this passage inconclusive. What is equally puzzling is the passage Nick gives us before he witnesses this scene: "A new point of view occurred to me. Suppose Tom found out that Daisy had been driving. He might think he saw a connection in it—he might think anything" (145). What can this possibly mean? What kind of a "connection" can Nick be thinking of here? Possibly that Daisy had intentionally run over Myrtle in order to get rid of her husband's lover? Possibly that his own name would become linked to Myrtle's in the event of an inquest? Whatever Nick is thinking here must remain speculative, and Fitzgerald leaves a narrative gap of immense proportions.

The ending of the novel is not much more helpful in answering some of these questions. Here Nick actually confronts Tom and asks him directly "what did you say to Wilson that afternoon?" (180). His question stems from a guess—a right guess—that Tom had sent Wilson in pursuit of Gatsby. But Tom insists that all he told Wilson was "the truth"; "'I told him the truth,' he said. 'He came to the door while we were getting ready to leave, and when I sent down word that we weren't in he tried to force his way upstairs. He was crazy enough to kill me if I hadn't told him who owned the car'" (180). So Tom tells Wilson that the death car was Gatsby's, but does he know when he tells Wilson this that Daisy was driving it? Tom implies that he did not know, and he concludes, "He [Gatsby] ran over Myrtle like you'd run over a dog and never even stopped his car" (180).

That Tom, of course, says this means nothing. He does not know that Nick knows from Gatsby that Daisy was driving, so his response to Nick is totally self-serving, and in character with Tom. What is more puzzling is Nick's response here. "There was nothing I could say, except the one unutterable fact that it wasn't true" (180). Why is this fact "unutterable"? If Tom knows that Daisy was driving, why not call his bluff? If he does not know, what is to be gained by allowing him to think that Gatsby had run over Myrtle? Would this information be more damaging to Tom and Daisy's marriage than what Tom already knows? Would this information really matter that much to Tom, now that Gatsby is dead and that Daisy has returned to him? The most that Nick's silence can do is to safeguard Tom's self-righteousness. Maybe that is why he holds his tongue. From Tom's point of view, Gatsby got what he deserved, whether Gatsby or Daisy was driving the car. "That fellow had it coming to him," Tom says to Nick, "He threw dust into your eyes just like he did in Daisy's" (180). There is probably not much point in arguing against logic like this. Tom has retreated into his "vast carelessness" and his "money" and is now insulated from moral arguments and "provincial squeamishness" (180–81). So in what can be taken as a gesture of defeat, an inability to ncture the moral self-righteousness of the high rich, Nick lets Tom off the hook: "I shook hands with him; it seemed silly not to, for I felt suddenly as though I were talking to a child" (181).

This ending of the novel makes the other "ending" all the more ambiguous. Many critics read Nick's leaving the East for the West as a moral triumph on his part. But Nick's "what's the use" attitude that he displays with Tom gives the impression of someone more beaten down by his experience than in moral control of it. This question becomes even more complex when it is put in the context of Nick's insistence to Gatsby that one cannot repeat the past. Given the nostalgic connection Nick makes between his childhood and the West, his retreat home seems to parallel Gatsby's desire to buy back the past as well as reaffirm the last words of the novel—that it is an American destiny to "beat on, boats against the current, borne back ceaselessly into the past" (182). We can well understand why Nick might be disillusioned with the East, why it might be distorted beyond his eye's power morally to correct. But is a retreat to the world of his father's hardware store the answer to this situation?

Unquestionably, Fitzgerald would not want the ending of his novel stated in these terms. From the beginning of the novel he had established a contrast between the West and the East, and by the time he gets to the ending, Nick can say, "I see now that this has been a story of the West, after all" (177). Nick goes on to catalog the characters who have come from the West, and then concludes, "perhaps we possessed some deficiency in common which made us subtly unadaptable to Eastern life" (177). With the exception of Tom Buchanan, who seems to embody the very meaning of the East, Nick's words have a ring of truth. As we have seen, Fitzgerald, like Frederick Jackson Turner, Van Wyck Brooks, and others, had come to believe that the center of gravity in America had shifted from West to East. Gatsby comes to the East, not to the frontier of Dan Cody or James J. Hill, but to the new megalopolis, the world of the high finance broker and the underworld king. In the dens of the underworld he stakes out his fortune, a fortune without social credentials, but vast enough, at least on the surface, to compete with Tom Buchanan's. For all the excitement that Nick feels as he walks the streets of New York trying to unlock the secrets and the mystery of the city, he comes to understand that such a world feeds on the labor

Careless Driving: Nick Carraway

and energy of others—like the Wilsons, that the city is both lure and prey, and that the lonely clerks walking the empty evening streets are all young romantics in the process of having their dreams drained. The image, like so much from *The Great Gatsby*, is right out of *The Waste Land*, and the ending of Fitzgerald's novel is the narrative equivalent of Eliot's Unreal City. Like Eliot's Tiresias, Nick's physical vision blurs and his inner vision becomes more acute, or so we are supposed to believe. But if that is the case, exactly what is the vision that Nick leaves us at the end? On second thought, that vision also seems a bit blurred. The West seems to call Nick not with a sense of radical new possibility (nowhere has the novel ever suggested this) but simply as an alternative to the East that Nick can no longer abide, an East that has lost contact with the simple and homely courtesies that Nick, like Fitzgerald, had come to associate with the West.

In coming to this conclusion Fitzgerald was perhaps most influenced by a contemporary novel, Willa Cather's *A Lost Lady*, which we know he read with deep interest, dealing with a topic so close to his own that he wrote Cather insisting that, despite the extraordinary similarity, he was not guilty of plagiarism. Nevertheless, the parallels between these texts are obvious and abundant. In *A Lost Lady* the meaning of the frontier is carried by Captain Forrester, who came to the plains after the Civil War and helped cut the railroad through that country. The spirit of the frontier is carried on by his young wife, Marian, who comes from California, marries the captain after he has had a serious accident, and becomes a symbol of all that is good to Niel Herbert, very much the Nick Carraway figure in the novel. Although Niel does not actually narrate the story, he establishes a moral presence that carries the meaning. His scorn becomes focused on Frank Ellinger, a kind of Tom Buchanan figure, who embodies the movement toward a world of force. Ellinger is even described in terms that resemble Tom:

Frank Ellinger was a bachelor of forty, six feet two, with long straight legs, fine shoulders, and a figure that still permitted his white waistcoat to button without a wrinkle under his conspicuously well-cut coat. His black hair, coarse and curly as the filling of a mattress, was grey about

107

the ears, his florid face showed little purple veins about his beaked nose,—a nose like the prow of a ship, with long nostrils. His chin was deeply cleft, his thick curly lips seemed very muscular, very much under his control, and, with his strong white teeth, irregular and curved, gave him the look of a man who could bite an iron rod in two with a snap of his jaws. His whole figure seemed very much alive under his clothes, with a restless, muscular energy that had something of the cruelty of wild animals in it.[32]

Although Tom is ten years younger than Ellinger, the physical details that Fitzgerald uses to describe Tom—the "hard mouth," the "arrogant eyes," his "aggressive" stance, "the enormous power" of his body that "not even the effeminate swank of his riding clothes could hide," the "glistening boots" packed with muscle, the "great pack of muscle shifting when his shoulder moved under his thin coat," the "enormous leverage" of that "cruel body" (7)—are remarkably similar.

Niel's moral scorn is also directed at Ivy Peters, whose cruelty and amoral, if not immoral, business acumen lead to the eventual making of a fortune. When Niel learns that Mrs. Forrester has had an affair with Ellinger and when he later discovers that she has turned over her business dealings to Peters, he is totally disillusioned. What Niel sees passing is a way of life that he equates with the West, a way of life that ends with the death of the captain and the corruption of Mrs. Forrester. The captain himself signals such a passing earlier in the novel:

> "Because a thing that is dreamed of in the way I mean, is already an accomplished fact. All our great West has been developed from such dreams; the homesteader's and the prospector's and the contractor's. We dreamed the railroad across the mountains, just as I dreamed my place on the Sweet Water. All these things will be everyday facts to the coming generation, but to us—" Captain Forrester ended with a sort of grunt. Something forbidding had come into his voice, the lonely, defiant note that is so often heard in the voices of old Indians. (Cather, 55).

In *The Great Gatsby* Nick speaks of Gatsby as unique, as one of a dying kind. He had "an extraordinary gift for hope, a romantic readiness such as I have never found in any other person and which it is not likely I shall ever find again" (2). Such intensity is inseparable from the vision that created America and that led generation after generation across an ocean and then across a continent until it exhausted the land and then turned back upon itself. Fitzgerald would treat this theme again in *The Last Tycoon*, as indeed Willa Cather had treated it in *A Lost Lady*. We are told at the end of Cather's novel that Niel "had seen the end of an era, the sunset of the pioneer. He had come upon it when already its glory was nearly spent. . . . This was the very end of the road-making West; the men who had put plains and mountains under the iron harness were old; some were poor, and even the successful ones were hunting for rest and a brief reprieve from death. It was already gone, that age; nothing could ever bring it back" (Cather, 168–69).

Niel can never forgive Mrs. Forrester for betraying the spirit of this vision, the same kind of vision that Gatsby brings East and contaminates with social pretense. He condemns Mrs. Forrester for not being "willing to immolate herself, like the widow of all these great men, and die with the pioneer period to which she belonged; that she preferred life on any terms" (Cather, 169). Mrs. Forrester can never come up to Niel's ideals because what he wants her ideally to embody is a dead past, which she refuses to do. Gatsby brings that dead past East and registers a more ambiguous response from Nick—an admiration for what was "gorgeous about him," for "his heightened sensitivity to the promises of life," and an "unaffected scorn" for the way Gatsby went about realizing such promise. Nick wants two contradictory things: he wants the intensity of the dream long after the reality of the dream has passed, and he wants romantic readiness after the romantic object has been exhausted of its meaning. When Nick leaves Gatsby, who is standing vigil at Daisy's house after the death of Myrtle Wilson, Nick tells us, "So I walked away and left him standing there in the moonlight—watching over nothing" (146). What he leaves us with is the nowhere hero, the Gatsby figure who stands between a dead past and an unrealizable future. When Nick retreats into the West at the end of the novel he seems to be going in search of the ideal vestiges of that dead past.

At the end of *A Lost Lady* Niel Herbert makes a last, disillusioned visit to Mrs. Forrester's house, now emptied of meaning. In *The Great*

Gatsby Nick leaves Gatsby maintaining an empty vigil at Daisy's house, and at the end of the novel Nick visits Gatsby's empty house under a moonlit sky and thinks of the moment when the pioneer vision came into being. When he returns West, it is to houses that still have personal names attached to them, to a world of homely comforts; perhaps that will be enough for Nick, although certainly the novel never tells us that. But what the novel does tell us in its last words seems to apply as much to Nick as to Gatsby: "So we beat on, boats against the current, borne back ceaselessly into the past" (182).

In *Gatsby* Fitzgerald showed a certain cultural materialism (embodied in Tom Buchanan) exhausting a romantic energy (embodied in Gatsby) leaving us a physical residue (embodied by George and Myrtle Wilson and the Valley of Ashes). Fitzgerald brilliantly showed how romantic expectation was connected with historical ideals always located in an exhausted past. By the time that we get to the end of the novel, when Fitzgerald would like to find the means of moral escape for Nick Carraway, he cannot convincingly send him to the romantic past because he was too successful as a novelist in showing that past to be empty. Nick strangely and ironically repeats Gatsby's search for an idealized past, and his return to the West is to an idealized world of childhood that no longer exists. What we have here is the opposite of how time works in a novel by Fielding or Dickens, which resolves the plot around a fixed moral center toward which that novel (that is, toward which time) moves. Fitzgerald empties time of such a moral ideal until the novel can no longer be recuperated around such a center. Such a process is a matter of narrative unfolding. Fitzgerald is asking what happens when an idea of self conceptualized in terms of the past (as embodied in Dan Cody and the idea of the frontier) is played out in the urban world of Tom Buchanan. Here the novel is clearly questioning its own moral center by showing the mechanics of power at work exploiting the vacuum of an exhausted past.

12

Seeing and Misseeing: Narrative Unfolding

> Even when the East excited me most, even when I was most keenly aware of its superiority to the bored, sprawling, swollen towns beyond the Ohio, with their interminable inquisitions which spared only the children and the very old—even then it had always for me a quality of distortion. West Egg, especially, still figures in my more fantastic dreams. . . .
> After Gatsby's death the East was haunted for me like that, distorted beyond my eyes' power of correction. (178–79)

Whatever may be Nick Carraway's inconsistencies, whatever may be the limitations of his character, two elements of his being help to redeem him: first, he is the only character in the novel with an interiority of self, the only character who internalizes this strange and fascinating world that makes up Fitzgerald's novel; and second, he is the only one in the novel who takes responsibility for Gatsby once he is dead. Nick, in fact, has so internalized Gatsby's story, has so identified with Gatsby, that he goes about preparing for Gatsby's funeral with a special kind of urgency. Gatsby dead still speaks to Nick, or rather Nick's projection of Gatsby's subjectivity speaks to him in an imploring way: "Look here, old sport, you've got to get somebody for me. You've got to try hard. I can't go through this alone" (166).

The novel is, of course, an exercise in retrospective narration. The events have already unfolded when Nick begins his story. Perhaps because the events that begin the novel seem so inseparable from the events that conclude it, we, as readers, feel a kind of inevitability built into Nick's story. From the very first paragraphs in which Nick talks about a world that falls short of his moral desires, about "what preyed on Gatsby, what foul dust floated in the wake of his dreams" (2), we know that all is not going to end well for Gatsby. The sequence of events in the novel are expertly foreshadowed as is Fitzgerald's symbolic use of time as the following chronology clearly shows.

CHAPTER 1

Autumn, 1922. Nick has returned home to the Midwest and begins telling the story of Gatsby, which he witnessed that summer.

Wednesday, 7 June 1922. Nick is invited to dinner by Tom and Daisy Buchanan. "In two weeks it'll be the longest day of the year" (12), Daisy tells us. Tom was Nick's classmate at Yale, and Daisy is his "second cousin once removed," which means that his grandfather, who "started the wholesale hardware business that my father carries on today," could be Daisy's grandfather. At the Buchanans' Nick meets Jordan Baker, who has been raised by an aunt, Mrs. Sigourney Howard. (At Newman Academy Fitzgerald's mentor was Father Cyril Sigourney Fay. Fitzgerald's naming his heroines after Father Fay was perhaps an inside joke, although in the slang of the time "fay" [fairy] also meant "otherworldly," suggesting the transcendent.)

CHAPTER 2

A following Sunday "a few days before the Fourth of July," which would make it Sunday, 2 July 1922, Nick goes into New York with Tom. On the way they pick up Myrtle Wilson, Tom's mistress, in the valley of ashes, and go to an apartment at 158th Street where Tom has been taking Myrtle to make love. What is significant about this date is that almost a month has passed (despite the fact this event follows immediately after the events of chapter 1) since Nick and Tom have been reacquainted, long enough to let Nick back into Tom's confidence when it comes to matters of illicit love. This is a good example of "gaps" or "pockets of silence" in the text that speak to us when we are reading carefully. Both Fitzgerald and Hemingway believed that the novelist could omit key information, as long as the novelist "knew"—that is, had imagined or conceptualized—what he was omitting.

CHAPTER 3

Saturday, 8 July 1922. Nick attends the first of the parties that Gatsby has been giving since the beginning of the summer. While the exact date here is a guess, it does fit the time scheme of the novel. It is probably a Saturday evening party because Gatsby's parties last the weekend and Gatsby has invited Nick, who works in New York on weekdays, out for a ride in his "hydroplane tomorrow morning [Sunday, 9 July] at nine o'clock" (53).

CHAPTER 4

"One morning late in July" (63) about six weeks after the Buchanan dinner party (79), which would place the date at approximately 19 July 1922, Nick and Gatsby motor in to New York in Gatsby's Rolls Royce where they later meet Meyer Wolfsheim for lunch "in a well-fanned Forty-second Street cellar" (69).

Later that afternoon "in a tea-garden at the Plaza Hotel" Jordan tells Nick the story of how Gatsby and Daisy met:

Retrospective Narration: *October 1917. Daisy Fay, eighteen, and Jay Gatsby, twenty-seven, have been meeting that summer in Louisville. Jordan is sixteen at the time. (Thus at the time the main action of the novel takes place, Gatsby is thirty-two, Daisy is twenty-three, and Jordan is twenty-one. Tom we know is thirty [7], and Nick turns thirty later that summer.) Gatsby has been stationed at Camp Taylor. He and Daisy will be separated in November 1917, so the retrospective story of Daisy and Gatsby parallels the time scheme of the main story: they meet in the* summer and are separated in the autumn. Early the next year Daisy's mother finds her packing her bag "one winter night to go to New York and say good-by to a soldier who was going overseas" (76). The soldier is, of course, Gatsby. The mother forestalls these plans. Although at first angry, Daisy was soon "gay again," and she makes her debut "after the Armistice" (11 November 1918). In February 1919 "she was presumably engaged to a man from New Orleans," but in June 1919 she married Tom Buchanan of Chicago, despite a letter from Gatsby, which brings on a drunken moment of hesitancy (76–77).

From June to August 1919 Daisy and Tom carry out "a three months' trip to the South Seas" (78). They return in August to Santa Barbara where, a week later, Tom is involved in an auto accident in which he "ripped a front wheel off his car" and in which the girl with him broke her arm.

"The next April" (1920), ten months after their marriage, Daisy gives birth to Pammy (78), after which the Buchanans go to France "for a year" (78). They return to Chicago presumably in the spring of 1921, where they move "with a fast crowd" (78). They are forced to leave Chicago because of one of Tom's indiscretions (132) and are settled in East Egg at the time Nick begins telling his story.

CHAPTER 5

Nick returns to West Egg the night that he meets Meyer Wolfsheim and talks to Jordan (82), presumably 19 July 1922, at which time he promises Gatsby that he will arrange a meeting between him and Daisy "The day after tomorrow" (83), which would mean this famous meeting took place on Friday, 21 July. At eleven o'clock in the morning of that rainy day a man in a raincoat comes to cut Nick's lawn; at two o'clock a "greenhouse" full of flowers arrives, and at three o'clock (the same hour that he will die) a highly nervous Gatsby arrives (84). At two minutes to four (85), despite Gatsby's skepticism, Daisy arrives. They have not seen each other since November 1917, a separation of four years and eight months or "five years next November" (88), as Gatsby knows all too well. Nick

114

leaves the reunited lovers for about "half an hour" (89). When he returns, they visit Gatsby's house and later "the grounds and the swimming-pool, and the hydroplane and the mid-summer flowers" (94), all testimony, Gatsby believes, to his newfound worth, the coin he is counting on to justify Daisy's love. After listening to Klipspringer play the piano, Nick says good-bye, dubious that Daisy can incarnate the ideal that Gatsby has created (97).

CHAPTER 6

Chapter 6 offers the first sustained account of Gatsby's origins. Nick interrupts the flow of the main narrative to give us an account of Gatsby's first meeting Dan Cody.

Retrospective Narration: *Gatsby, as we know, is thirty-two in 1922 and thus was born in 1890. Since he meets Dan Cody at the age of seventeen, that year has to be 1907, ten years before Gatsby becomes involved with Daisy. His meeting with Cody and his love for Daisy are the two elements that determine his conception of self. Gatsby is born in North Dakota, attends St. Olaf's College in southern Minnesota for "two weeks," and then drifts to Lake Superior, where he meets Cody, who is fifty years old at the time, "a product of the Nevada silver fields, of the Yukon, of every rush for metal since seventy-five" (100). He made millions "many times" over in Montana copper (100) before he became involved with the unsavory newspaper woman Ella Kaye in 1902. He had thus "been coasting along all too hospitable shores for five years" (100) when he comes sailing in his ship the* Tuolomee *into James Gatz's life at Little Girl Bay. Gatsby travels "three times around the Continent" with Cody for five years—from 1907 to 1912—as "steward, mate, skipper, secretary, and even jailor" (101), until he is displaced by Ella Kaye in Boston a week before Cody dies. Cody left Gatsby a legacy of $25,000 which "he didn't get" (101), thanks to the scheming of Miss Kaye. Instead Cody left him a "singularly appropriate education" (102). What Gatsby does for the next five years—that is, until he appears on Daisy's doorsteps in 1917—the text never explicitly tells us.*

Several weeks pass in the summer of 1922 that Nick spends "mostly . . . in New York, trotting around with Jordan and trying to ingratiate myself with her senile aunt" (102). Nick calls on Gatsby "one Sunday afternoon" (102), 13 August, at which time Tom, a Mr. Sloane, and an unidentified woman stop by on horses.

"The following Saturday night" (105), 19 August, Gatsby gives the second party that Nick attends. Daisy and Tom also make an appearance, and Daisy is "appalled by West Egg, this unprecedented 'place' that Broadway had begotten upon a Long Island fishing village" (108), at which point Gatsby closes his house and ends "his career as Trimalchio" (113).

CHAPTER 7

When the lights in Gatsby's house fail to go on "one Saturday," Nick journeys over to discover the house has been taken over by unfamiliar help, some with "villainous" faces and Wolfsheim connections (113–14). The next day, a Sunday, Gatsby calls Nick on the phone and tells him he wanted servants "who wouldn't gossip. Daisy comes over quite often—in the afternoon" (114). Gatsby and later Daisy herself invite Nick for lunch the next day at the Buchanan house. "The next day," it turns out, "was broiling, almost the last, certainly the warmest, of the summer" (114). We know from this passage and the fact that Nick works until noon this Monday, that the date cannot be 4 September, Labor Day, but must come two weeks later, which would literally make it "almost the last . . . [day] of the summer." Thus on Monday, 18 September 1922, a little more than three months after Nick first visits the Buchanans, he returns again, supposedly to witness Daisy making a public break with Tom and professing her love openly for Gatsby. Despite the fact that it is a workday, the group is looking for "something to do." They travel into New York in the late afternoon and stop for bootlegged drinks at a suite in the Plaza Hotel, where Daisy's intended break with Tom fails once she learns the source of Gatsby's money.

It is seven o'clock when Daisy and Gatsby in one car and Nick, Jordan, and Tom in another start back to Long Island. This is the hour of dusk, the hour the twelve men of Fish watch the sun go down, as it is doing in the valley of ashes when Daisy runs over Myrtle Wilson. Gatsby drives his car to his garage in West Egg and then takes Daisy home in a taxi (181). Tom, who has stopped at the accident, arrives shortly thereafter. Now at dark, Nick sees Gatsby emerge from the bushes and later witnesses the Buchanans "conspiring together" at the kitchen table, before he taxis to West Egg, leaving Gatsby standing "vigil" in the moonlight "over nothing" (146).

CHAPTER 8

The next day, Tuesday, 19 September, Gatsby arrives by taxi in West Egg. He had waited until "about four o'clock" in the morning at Daisy's. From this time until dawn Gatsby and Nick talk.

Retrospective Narration: *Gatsby tells Nick the story of how he fell in love with Daisy, including the fact that "he took Daisy one still October [1917] night," leaving Gatsby "nothing," except a feeling that he was "married to her" (149). After the war, like a religious pilgrim, Gatsby makes a sacred journey back to Louisville, to the shrine where their love was "consummated" and his love for Daisy "incarnated" (152–53). The religious imagery Fitzgerald so explicitly gives to Gatsby's love for Daisy parallels the religious journey of the Pilgrims to the New World and the intensity of vision of the Dutch sailors who first see the shores of this virginal world. Fitzgerald's language works to make such connections, in this case the connection between the sexual destiny of Gatsby and the national destiny of America.*

Gatsby and Nick eat breakfast and Nick leaves for New York in the late morning. "Just before noon" he talks with Jordan by phone. He tries to call Gatsby but Gatsby's phone is "being kept open for long distance from Detroit" (156). Nick takes the 3:50 P.M. train back to West Egg.

At this point in the narrative Nick gives us an account of what happened the night before in George Wilson's garage. How exactly he gets this information, the text never makes clear. After Myrtle's death, Wilson is consoled by Michaelis, who leaves him when another "watcher" arrives at 6:00 A.M. At 10:00 A.M. Michaelis goes back to the garage and Wilson is gone. Wilson, Nick speculates, reaches Gad's Hill at noon. He then "disappears" for three hours, which Nick discovers later involved him going first to Tom Buchanan's house and then, believing from Tom that it was Gatsby who killed Myrtle, moving on to Gatsby's. At 2:00 P.M. Gatsby heads for his pool. At 2:30 Wilson is in West Egg asking directions to Gatsby's house. At 3:00 P.M. on Tuesday, 19 September 1922, Wilson finds Gatsby floating on a pneumatic mattress in his pool and kills him with a revolver shot before he turns the gun on himself.

CHAPTER 9

Two years have elapsed since Gatsby's death, placing Nick's final words to us in the autumn of 1924 (164), at the time that Fitzgerald himself had reached this point in the story.

The day after Gatsby is killed, 20 September 1922, Nick takes on the responsibility of arranging for Gatsby's funeral.

On 21 September he sends a butler to New York with a letter for Wolfsheim.

"On the third day," 22 September, a telegram arrives from Gatsby's father, Henry C. Gatz, who is on the way to New York and requests the funeral be postponed until he arrives (167). He arrives on the 24th, for the "funeral tomorrow" (170). Gatsby is thus buried on Monday 25 September.

The morning of the funeral (171) Nick calls on Wolfsheim, who tells him that he shows "friendship for a man when he is alive and not after he is dead" (173). Nick returns to find Mr. Gatz with Gatsby's copy of *Hopalong Cassidy* inscribed with Benjamin Franklin–like resolves and dated 12 September 1906. (Since this novel was not published until 1910, Gatsby could not have dated it in 1906.) "A little before three" (175) a

Lutheran minister arrives and at "five o'clock" (175) the procession of three cars reached the cemetery where, shortly after, Gatsby is buried in the rain. Thus the rain that falls on the reunion of Gatsby and Daisy seems to harbinger the rain that falls on his burial.

Some time in early autumn, "when the blue smoke of brittle leaves was in the air and the wind blew the wet laundry stiff on the line" (178), Nick decides to head back West. Before he leaves, he breaks with Jordan Baker, and "one afternoon late in October" (179) he has his final confrontation with Tom Buchanan. His last night in the East is spent in the moonlight at Gatsby's mansion, thinking of the first sailor to see the shores of America, who, like Gatsby, was "compelled into aesthetic contemplation . . . face to face for the last time in history with something commensurate to his capacity for wonder" (182).

●   ●   ●

Both structurally and chronologically, *The Great Gatsby* builds toward chapter 5, the scene in which Gatsby again meets Daisy after their long separation. In a nine-chapter novel, this is the exact halfway point; the first four chapters build toward this moment, and the last four chapters lead away from it. Fitzgerald seems to have had this plan in mind from the outset, although he did make some important changes in his holograph version of the novel, now published as "A Facsimile of the Manuscript." The most important change involves the reversal of what are chapters 2 and 3 of the novel. In the holograph version chapter 2 treats Gatsby's party, and chapter 3 treats Gatsby's calling on Nick, recounting the "story" of his career, and driving Nick into New York where they lunch with Wolfsheim, closing with Jordan's retrospective account as witness to Gatsby's and Daisy's love. Another chapter, also confusedly labeled chapter 3 in the holograph, treats the Wilsons, and moves us from the valley of ashes to the party with Myrtle, her sister, and the McKees in the apartment Tom keeps for his lovemaking. Whereas the novel ends this chapter with Nick "half asleep" waiting for the four o'clock train in Pennsylvania Station (38), this chapter in the holograph ends with Nick's reflections on New York, on the character of Jordan Baker, and on his own honesty. Fitzgerald will later move this section up to chapter 3 and use it as the conclusion to the scene at Gatsby's party.

Why Fitzgerald chose to put the scene with Tom and Myrtle Wilson before the scene at the party is worth a moment of contemplation. Unless one is paying close attention to the time element of the novel as discussed above, it does seem a bit strained that Tom would take Nick so quickly into his confidence and invite him to a moment of his lovemaking with Myrtle. And yet this scene intensifies the image of Tom as the arrogant bully that we get in chapter 1. Moreover, by delaying the appearance of Gatsby until chapter 3, the mystery surrounding him is intensified. Fitzgerald thus restructured his first version of the novel to have the first four chapters work as "pairs," chapters 1 and 2 giving us a sustained look at Tom, a character who Fitzgerald was afraid at one point might run away with the novel, and chapters 3 and 4 giving us our first sustained look at Gatsby, leading now more smoothly to chapter 5, the all-important moment of reunion. In the holograph version he also ended chapter 1 with the famous passage about the Dutch sailors first seeing the shores of America. Thus we see that this key theme was in his mind from the outset and that this passage was so important that it should come at the end of the whole novel. Fitzgerald's narrative instincts were completely unerring. The final unfolding of these events as we have them in the published novel builds by establishing the brutality and arrogance of Tom, then reveals the mystery of Gatsby's background and the intensity of his romantic vision of self, while it firmly locates Nick as a bridge between the two as well as a participant, because of his relationship with Jordan Baker, in the action itself—all of which moves us to the crucial center of the novel, the reunion of Gatsby and Daisy.

Chapter 5, the reunion scene, is the static center of the novel. Here time past and time present fuse; the dream comes as close to incarnation as it is possible for it to come. Fitzgerald infuses this section with time images and references. This symbolic intensity belies the physical reality of the scene, and Fitzgerald later admitted that he did not really know what Daisy's response to Gatsby would or should be. Fitzgerald found a way out of this narrative dilemma by making the response as vague and general as possible. He equated their love with the grotesque magnificence of Gatsby's house; Daisy is clearly moved by a man who could love her with such an intensity that it would redirect his whole life; and Fitzgerald finds a kind of romantic equivalent for that sense of fidelity—a fidelity clearly counterpointed by Tom's constant infidelity—in Gatsby's splendid array of silk shirts, which literally move Daisy to tears.

Fitzgerald's instinct here to substitute romantic symbols for realistic character motives was probably right. Given his inventiveness, it is always dangerous to deny him narrative alternatives, but it does seem difficult to believe that he could have romanticized the rather seamy aftermath of the Gatsby-Daisy reunion; after all, this is a novel about double adultery, about a fatal auto accident, about murder and suicide. The romantic aura of Fitzgerald's novel belies the current of violence that runs beneath it; the grotesque underside of the novel is always threatening to overpower the romantic core, as it does poetically at the end when (Nick conjectures) Gatsby's romantic vision turns the old warm world into an unfamiliar sky, frightening leaves, and a grotesque rose; and as it does for Nick when West Egg becomes the surreal equivalent of a drunken woman in a white evening dress, bedecked with jewels (all reminiscent of Gatsby's parties), being carried on a stretcher by four men (like pallbearers) into the wrong house (178). The imagery here recapitulates the novel, especially the way the romantic moment grotesquely undoes itself. The glamour of Gatsby's parties turns into drunken affairs; a sense of wealth and well-being turns into sickness and death; and the surreal swirl of houses and events robs Nick of focus and stability.

After chapter 5 the rest of the novel seems to unfold in this way. Chapter 6, the second Gatsby party, turns rancid under Daisy's scorn. The narrative momentum moves us to chapter 7, the confrontation scene—upon which the resolution of the novel turns—at the Plaza Hotel, followed by the death of Myrtle Wilson, which prefigures in chapter 8 the death of Gatsby. Chapter 9, the funeral of Gatsby, serves as a kind of coda, Nick's summary statement. Over and over, the desire for the resplendent gives way to the grotesque or to violence. The lovely ambience of the Buchanan's dinner party gives way to the ugliness of Tom's casual love affairs, already beginning to spill into public recognition; the humorous airs of Myrtle give way to the somberness of Tom's breaking her nose; the carnival-like good time at Gatsby's first party gives way to a drunken auto accident at the end; the drinking party at the Plaza ends with the defeat of Gatsby and the death of Myrtle and later of Gatsby. And not only does the romantic moment seem to have the grotesque and tragic embedded in it, but one scene seems to anticipate, sometimes ironically, another, and the novel seems to unfold in paired scenes: for example, two Gatsby parties; two scenes at the Buchanans', one whipped by a cool wind, the other oppressed by a summer heat; Nick has lunch with Wolfsheim in New York and later visits his office; Nick takes Jordan to tea at the Plaza, where the pivotal scene in the novel will later take place.

Not only does the romantic moment seem to unfold toward violence, but it does so with a recurring sense of blindness. This is a novel about seeing and misseeing. Nick sees but does not recognize Jordan at the beginning of the novel; the Washington Heights party turns into a drunken blur before Nick's eyes, a little like the blurred "portrait" McKee has of his mother-in-law on the wall; Nick fails to recognize Gatsby even as he speaks to him at Gatsby's first party; Wolfsheim mistakes Nick for one of Gatsby's underworld "gonnegtions" when they first meet in the Broadway restaurant. But the most important moment of seeing/misseeing takes place when Tom, Jordan, and Nick drive into Wilson's gas station on their way to New York that fatal September day, and Myrtle looks out from the upper room window, where Wilson is literally keeping her prisoner, and mistakes Jordan for Daisy and—more important—Gatsby's car for Tom's. The blindness of this perception is clearly connected with the spirit of blindness that runs through the novel. When Nick becomes aware of Myrtle's presence, it is only after he tells us: "Over the ashheaps the giant eyes of Doctor T. J. Eckleburg kept their vigil, but I perceived, after a moment, that other eyes were regarding us with peculiar intensity from less than twenty feet away" (124–25). Because of this confusion, when Daisy and Gatsby are driving back to East Egg from New York, Myrtle will run into the road, thinking Tom is in the yellow car, to implore his help against Wilson. She sees, but she missees, as does Wilson when he comes to believe that Gatsby is Myrtle's lover, and so does Wilson again when he believes that Gatsby was driving the car that killed his wife. Just before Wilson leaves on his fatal mission of murder, he looks into the "eyes of Doctor T. J. Eckleburg, which had just emerged, pale and enormous, from the dissolving night," and tells us, "God sees everything," and then proceeds to kill the wrong person (160). Fitzgerald's romantic world unfolds with a kind of blindness toward violence and the grotesque. The reality of this narrative fact is belied by Nick, who tells us from the beginning that what he wants most is a world of moral absolutes, the world in uniform and at a sort of moral attention forever (2). What Nick wants, of course, is the order that only an all-seeing, beneficent God can give to the world. As we know, Fitzgerald had intended at one time to write a novel about the Gilded Age set in New York with a Catholic element. While he never wrote that novel, *The Great Gatsby* in many ways conceptualizes some of these ideas. As in Van Wyck Brooks's interpretation of Mark Twain's ordeal, Fitzgerald believed that the frontier had been corrupted and then the center of gravity had moved to the city, especially such an eastern city as New York. There a surface world of genteel values (eventually the world of the Buchanans) covered economic corruption.

Henry James had given us an insight into this world. There was no real moral center to it; his characters substituted their subjectivity for such a moral center; and the resolution of a James novel often shows them retreating into an interior world of their own moral values. Fitzgerald gives this narrative pattern another turn and makes Nick's own subjectivity also morally problematic. What Nick wants morally, he is never able to get in a world where the values of East and West cancel each other out in the name of Tom Buchanan. Nick wants the world at moral attention, but what he gets are the blind eyes of Dr. Eckleburg, embodied by the owl-eyed man (a kind of American Tiresias) and by his own myopia, his inability to bring the world he is describing into focus.

In *The Great Gatsby* Fitzgerald brilliantly shows the moral breakdown of two visions—the pioneer vision of America, and Gatsby's vision of Daisy. This breakdown undoes the possibility of any kind of moral center, even a center as subjective as Nick's own sense of inner reality. The East, he tells us, was corrupted for him, "distorted beyond my eyes' power of correction" (178). The center cannot hold, and romantic possibility gives way to a corrupt reality. The green breast of the new world—

the uncorrupted frontier—gives way to the valley of ashes; the dream of
an idealized love gives way to adultery and death; and the idea of a just
God gives way to blind eyes overlooking a physical wasteland and to
characters who continually missee when they see at all.

13

A Blanket of Prose: Style and Meaning

The worst fault in [*The Great Gatsby*], I think is a BIG FAULT: I gave no account (and had no feeling about or knowledge of) the emotional relations between Gatsby and Daisy from the time of their reunion to the catastrophe. However, the lack is so astutely concealed by the retrospect of Gatsby's past and by blankets of excellent prose that no one has noticed it—tho everyone has felt the lack and called it by another name.—

letter from Fitzgerald to Edmund Wilson, spring 1925

When Fitzgerald began writing *The Great Gatsby*, he had a number of narrative modes from which he could choose. He could have followed the tradition of Zola and written in the vein of Norris and Dreiser as he had done in *The Beautiful and Damned*. Or he could have followed Flaubert and worked in the tradition of the aesthetic novel. Fitzgerald chose the latter path. Flaubert, of course, was not his principal model, but he influenced the idea of the aesthetic novel as it was transformed theoretically by Arthur Symons and Walter Pater and then radically honed by Joseph Conrad. An intermediary step in this process was the novel of Henry James—a novel, at least in the mid and later works of James, held together by an aesthetic consciousness as it dealt with cultural transformation, especially between Europe and America. But once again, Fitzgerald's instincts did not take him directly to James. In the critical debate between James and H. G. Wells that ended with Wells's attack on James in *Boon*, Fitzgerald was more sympathetic to Wellsian than to Jamesian fiction. What he wanted was a substantial story line, held together by an interesting narrative consciousness, and brought to a boil through symbolic use of language. He had made such intentions clear in his own comments on *The Great Gatsby*. He wrote Thomas Boyd, for example, "I shall never write another document-novel. I have decided to be a pure artist and experiment in form and emotion" (March 1923).[33] And he wrote Maxwell Perkins before he had begun his novel: "I want to write something *new*—something extraordinary and beautiful and simple and intricately patterned" (July 1922).[34]

Perhaps the work that most influenced Fitzgerald's imagination and helped him achieve these artistic aims was Eliot's *The Waste Land*. We have already discussed the similarity of themes, of narrative angle (the Tiresias figures), and even of phrasing between Eliot's poem and Fitzgerald's novel. But it is equally important to see that *The Waste Land* made use of a kind of narrative resonance, of stylistic reverberations, of interlocking patterns of language that are in great part responsible for the power of the poem—a power that a reader intuits or feels rather than consciously re-creates. Once Fitzgerald had decided that he was going to write a kind of poetic novel—the prose equivalent of *The Waste Land* —he was locked into a language system that would dictate his whole sense of craft.

Fitzgerald was working close to what Eliot meant by "objective correlative"—the belief that an author needed to create an objective equivalent to a narrative emotion so that the theme and meaning of a work could be carried by imagery and symbols, the reader abstracting from such language the thematic import of the work. Once this kind of work has been done successfully—and there is no better example than *The Great Gatsby*—it becomes very difficult to separate language and theme, and even theme from theme, because the language reverberates so powerfully that all of these matters become infused and interconnected. While this study has sought to separate some of the key themes in *The Great Gatsby*, particularly as they relate to the meanings of character and action, any such discussion will be successful only if it deepens the reader's awareness and allows the reader to reconstruct the novel in ways that will go far beyond this particular discussion. Every critical reading is a partial reading of a text, especially a text as complex as *Gatsby*; but every reading can become more deeply informed once one is aware of how a text is working within itself.

As this study has argued, Fitzgerald was working within terms of several broad themes in this novel. One involves the theme of America, the initial sense of promise of the New World as it was played out on the frontier and transformed by the new megalopolis. A second involves the theme of love and romance, embodied in Daisy Fay and played out and transformed in her five years of marriage with Tom Buchanan. A third, of course, involves Gatsby himself, his internalizing these themes—first, by modeling himself on Dan Cody and, second, by making his reunion with Daisy inseparable from the idea of self. As narrator, Nick Carraway becomes engrossed in the meaning of these matters and creates a story that only does partial justice to its complexity—as, indeed, our own reading will only do partial justice to such complexity. Like concentric circles spreading in a ruffled pond, these key elements begin to expand and aggregate, creating subsidiary themes, which in turn create more subsidiary themes. Connected with the theme of the frontier and the romantic self, for example, are themes of the lost past, of technology and the machine, of moral blindness, of waste and lost promise, just to recount a few. Once these and other key themes are infused with language, they take on a momentum of their own, move and merge into each other with a kind of pinwheel effect. To see this involves turning to the language of the text. There are a multitude of ways of talking about the language of a text like *The Great Gatsby* but consistent with the emphases of this study, we can perhaps limit our discussion to three elements: 1) language and theme, 2) language and association, and 3) language and foreshadowing.

A thematic study of language takes us to key expository passages in the novel, where such themes are given summary statements. The three most important passages in this context involve, first, Nick's connecting the vision of Gatsby with that of the Dutch sailors:

> And as the moon rose higher the inessential houses began to melt away until gradually I became aware of the old island here that flowered once for the Dutch sailors' eyes—a fresh green breast of the new world. (182)

The second such passage involves the moment Gatsby allows Daisy to incarnate the dream:

> Out of the corner of his eye Gatsby saw that the blocks of the side-
> walks really formed a ladder and mounted to a secret place above the
> trees—he could climb to it, if he climbed alone, and once there he
> could suck on the pap of life, gulp down the incomparable milk of
> wonder.
>   His heart beat faster and faster as Daisy's white face came up to
> his own. He knew that when he kissed this girl, and forever wed his
> unutterable visions to her perishable breath, his mind would never
> romp again like the mind of God. . . . Then he kissed her. At his lips'
> touch she blossomed for him like a flower and the incarnation was
> complete. (112)

The third passage involves the moment that Gatsby gives birth to himself
in his imagination:

> His parents were shiftless and unsuccessful farm people—his imagina-
> tion had never really accepted them as his parents at all. The truth was
> that Jay Gatsby of West Egg, Long Island, sprang from his Platonic
> conception of himself. He was a son of God. . . . So he invented just
> the sort of Jay Gatsby that a seventeen-year-old boy would be likely to
> invent, and to this conception he was faithful to the end. (99)

It is important to see that these passages not only state key themes in
an expository way, but they are also interconnected, and interconnect
with many other passages in the novel as well, through the associational
power of Fitzgerald's words. The "flowering" image of passage no. 1
("the old island here that flowered once for the Dutch sailors' eyes") obviously interconnects with the whole idea of Daisy as a kind of flower, as
her name suggests, and thus in passage no. 2 with the kiss, whereupon
Daisy "blossomed . . . like a flower." The green breast of the new world
finds a multitude of associations; it is meant to contrast with the valley of
ashes; to complement Gatsby, who, as we see in passage no. 2, drinks of
"the pap of life"; and to suggest the death of Myrtle, who is torn open by
the impact of the car so that "her left breast was swinging loose like a
flap" (138). The "moon" that bathes Gatsby's house in passage no. 1 is
the same moon that shone on Gatsby at the beginning of the novel (21),
as he waves good-bye to his guests after the first party (56), and as he

stands vigil at Daisy's window after the fatal auto accident (146). If Tom Buchanan is often associated with the sun (cf.118), Gatsby is continually associated with the moon. The moon not only gets its light from the sun (cf. the crooked broker theme) but is a romantic inversion of the sun symbol. And, in passage no. 2, it is under such a moon that Gatsby climbs a metaphorical ladder to the stars, and weds Daisy to his very idea of self. Such an act partakes of the godhead, as passage no. 3 makes abundantly clear, a passage that thus infuses additional meaning into the word *incarnation* in passage no. 2. And this sense of godlike capacity finds its ironic equivalent in the blind god that rules over the valley of ashes and the moral emptiness into which most of the narrative action falls.

Such examples—with their associative power—could be multiplied. The theme of the lost past, for one, is expanded by reference to overwound clocks (93), and by reference to the declining seasons of the year: the novel begins in late spring and ends in the autumn; within this cycle the story of Gatsby meeting Daisy also begins in the summer and ends in autumn. (This theme is intensified further in the holograph, where Gatsby's second party involves the celebration of the harvesting, and many of the guests are dressed in farmer costumes and hay is spread over the floor.) The theme of the lost past is inseparable from the theme of romantic exhaustion and lost promise, symbolized in the novel by ash heaps and dust imagery. When Myrtle Wilson, "her life violently extinguished, knelt in the road and mingled her thick dark blood with the dust" (138), the language fuses both religious and romantic meaning, perhaps in the case of Myrtle ironically so. Tom's remark at the end— Gatsby "threw dust into your eyes" (180)—not only picks up the dust/ashes imagery, but connects it with the theme of seeing/misseeing. That Wilson, the custodian of the valley of ashes, an "ashen, fantastic figure" (162), murders the green dreamer, Gatsby, is an irony too obvious to belabor. And the violence of Myrtle's death cannot be separated from the many auto references that thread through the novel and that connect to the theme of bad driving and moral carelessness, a note on which Nick closes the story (180). Thus passages weave and interweave with each other through this novel. Green lights on the end of docks suggests a green—and unexplored—America, suggest the promise of lovers' reunion, suggest money, and eventually suggest all of these matters at once. To discuss them critically involves sequence whereas, in the act of reading, something closer to simultaneity is the case.

Often built into the language of association is a language of fore-shadowing and anticipation. Images not only are superimposed upon each other, but they also begin to foreshadow key events in the novel. Near the end of chapter 3 the owl-eyed man steps from a car "violently shorn of one wheel" (54); near the end of chapter 4 we are told that Tom is involved in an automobile accident outside of Santa Barbara in which he "ripped a front wheel off his car" (78); and near the end of chapter 7 Myrtle Wilson is killed by an automobile. In chapter 5 rain falls on the reunion of Gatsby and Daisy; and in chapter 9 rain falls on Gatsby's fu-neral. In chapter 1 Daisy and Jordan sit on a couch that seems to float to the ceiling; in chapter 7 they sit on the same couch oppressed with heat, as if the airiness of their being has finally come down to earth, the spirit-ual has turned material, the transcendent earthly and grotesque, which is indeed what happens to Gatsby's vision by novel's end (cf. 162). The car-nival gaiety of Gatsby's party in chapter 3 disintegrates in chapter 6 under the disapproving eye of Daisy (an image that was used on the dust jacket of the first edition). And the city that Nick sees in its "wild promise of all the mystery and the beauty in the world" (69) gives way to the reality of death in chapter 4 ("A dead man passed us in a hearse heaped with blooms"). And in chapter 7 Nick will once again pass "over the dark bridge" and then drive "on toward death" (136–37).

The eggs in the Columbus story (5) harbinger the consummation of the Daisy-Gatsby love in October (Columbus Day), and harbinger in turn the sight of the New World corrupted by novel's end, just as the betrayal of the frontier is anticipated by Nick playing the "guide, a pathfinder, an original settler" (4). Dan Cody appears in Gatsby's life when he is fifty, and so does Meyer Wolfsheim; the femme fatale Ella Kaye seems (as the similarity in names suggest) to anticipate Daisy Fay; and the journeys of Columbus and later the Dutch sailors seemingly anticipate the death mat-tress that carries Gatsby's body in circles "like the leg of transit" (that is, compass) and that leaves "a thin red circle in the water" (163) like the three times Gatsby circles the continent with Dan Cody.

A Blanket of Prose: Style and Meaning

The copy of Clay's *Economics* that Nick buys at the beginning of the novel is the book Gatsby reads while he waits for Daisy (85), an appropriate choice in a novel where the heroine's "voice is full of money" (120). The "rose" referred to at the beginning of the novel (15) seems to foreshadow the grotesque rose Gatsby is left with at the end (162). The "almost pastoral" city we see at the beginning of the novel (28) belies the urban racketeering and the violence that eventually emerge. The owl-eyed man's appearance at the party seems to ensure his appearance at Gatsby's funeral. The out-of-date timetable that Nick uses to write the names of Gatsby's guests anticipates the obsolescence of Gatsby's dream. The eyes that blur the Washington Heights party for Nick foreshadow the eyes that blur for him after Gatsby's death, leaving the East "haunted . . . distorted beyond my eyes' power of correction" (178). The $350,000 string of pearls Tom gives Daisy before their wedding (77) is on the surface unconnected to Meyer Wolfsheim's cufflinks made of human molars (73), until the end of the novel, when Nick leaves Tom Buchanan at a jewelry store where he goes "to buy a pearl necklace—or perhaps only a pair of cuff buttons" (181). The words Wolfsheim speaks to Nick in the restaurant—"Gatsby's very careful about women. He would never so much as look at a friend's wife" (73)—reverberate with irony. And the words that Myrtle speaks when she first meets Tom—"You can't live forever; you can't live forever" (36)—take on an ironic chill by the time we get to the end of the novel. While the language of *The Great Gatsby* works in powerfully associative ways, it also works to foreshadow and anticipate the key scenes. Few other novels are so intricately patterned.

Once one understands how the language in *Gatsby* works, one is much better able to determine how the novel should be read—and not read. The symbolic language obviously undercuts a strict literal and realistic reading of this text. Thus the chronology we have worked out in our discussion of narration must not be taken too literally. While one can construct a time scheme from the text that helps explain the sequence of the important events that make up the novel, the symbolic relationships of that unfolding are more important than a strict knowledge of chronology. Movement from summer to winter, from youth to early adulthood, from romantic expectation to disillusionment, from life to death, from pastoral to tragic, from the ideal to the grotesque, from the spiritual to the material—these patterns are held together and facilitated by a well-wrought style that restricts our need to ask specific questions about character motives.

As narrator, Nick has all kinds of information that it is unlikely he would have. We never know how he has the detailed knowledge of what transpired in Wilson's garage prefatory to Gatsby's death. It also seems implausible that Gatsby, who three times circled the continent with Dan Cody, would not know the location of San Francisco (65). And we should probably not pursue too closely the logic of the story Gatsby tells Nick involving the death of Myrtle. To be sure, Daisy is driving, but Gatsby does manage to stop the car with the emergency brake. What need we make of the fact that he does have the option of returning to the scene of the accident? As Gatsby tells Nick, Daisy "fell over into my lap and I drove on" (145)—a statement that can surely compromise our sense of Gatsby's innocence, if we let it.

Poetic prose does not always hold up firmly under realistic scrutiny. To my mind, the weakest criticism of *Gatsby* involves readings that over-particularize the novel, robbing it of its romantic aura. To argue that Nick is a homosexual,[35] for example, overparticularizes the scene at the end of Myrtle's party where Nick, who has been moving with drunken randomness all evening long, finds himself standing beside Mr. McKee who, "sitting up between the sheets, clad in his underwear" is showing him a portfolio of his "art" work, photographs entitled "Beauty and the Beast," "Loneliness," "Old Grocery Horse," "Brooklyn Bridge" (38). To read this scene as other than a comic counterpart to a later tragic blurriness, to see something sinister going on between Nick and McKee, is to distort narrative unfolding, the way language works in this novel, and to impute motives to Nick that otherwise have no bearing—no other connection—in the novel at all.

Many other modern novels treat themes similar to those in *The Great Gatsby*. The pursuit of the romantic can be found in a similar way in the novels of Hermann Hesse, a writer who also influenced Eliot, as the footnotes to *The Waste Land* reveal; romantic disillusionment was often the major theme of H. G. Wells; Ford Madox Ford treats the passing of an old culture and the emptying of the historical moment in *The Good Soldier*, a novel that has been connected to *Gatsby*.[36] But as important as these works are, they lack the stylistic complexity of *The Great Gatsby*. Fitzgerald learned much from his most important mentor, Joseph Conrad, and a reading of *Lord Jim*, *Heart of Darkness*, and "Youth" can shed a kind of sideward light on *Gatsby*, as a number of critics have shown. But even Conrad, as great as he was, never went stylistically beyond what Fitzgerald accomplished in *The Great Gatsby*. Despite the flaws—"blemishes" is perhaps a better word—that we have recounted in this study, *Gatsby* is a singular novel, a major narrative achievement.

Fitzgerald seemed totally aware of that achievement. He was bereaved when the novel went out of print in his lifetime, despite the fact that he tried desperately to keep it alive. And the last novel of his life, the incomplete *The Last Tycoon*, was a return to the narrative mode of *Gatsby*, a highly controlled novel, narrated by a participating observer, intensified by symbolic imagery and language, which the unfinished text somewhat belies because such intensification came for Fitzgerald in the revising process.

Near the end of his life Fitzgerald seems to have much of this in his mind as he writes his daughter in the summer (12 June 1940) of the year in which he would die:

> What little I have accomplished has been by the most laborious and uphill work, and I wish now I'd *never* relaxed or looked back—but said at the end of *The Great Gatsby*: "I've found my line—from now on this comes first. This is my immediate duty—without this I am nothing." (*Letters*, 79)

NOTES

1. *The Great Gatsby* (New York: Scribner's, 1925; Scribner's Library edition, 1957), 47; hereafter cited in the text.

2. "Show Mr. and Mrs. F. to Number—," *Esquire,* May–June 1934; reprinted in *The Crack-Up,* ed. Edmund Wilson (New York: New Directions, 1945), 50.

3. The Notebooks of F. Scott Fitzgerald, ed. Matthew J. Bruccoli (New York: Harcourt Brace Jovanovich/Bruccoli Clark, 1978).

4. *Dear Scott/Dear Max,* ed. Jackson Bryer and John Kuehl (New York: Scribner's, 1971), 61.

5. Ibid., 70.

6. *Correspondence of F. Scott Fitzgerald,* ed. Matthew J. Bruccoli and Margaret M. Duggan (New York: Random House, 1980), 112.

7. Joseph Conrad, *The Nigger of the Narcissus* (New York: Dell, 1960), 26.

8. *The Stories of F. Scott Fitzgerald,* ed. Malcolm Cowley (New York: Scribner's, 1951), 164; hereafter cited in the text as *Stories.*

9. Ibid., 7.

10. James R. Mellow argues in *Invented Lives* (Boston: Houghton Mifflin, 1984) that Fitzgerald used the name of a real-life acquaintance. That may be so (Fitzgerald also used the name of Sigourney Fay in his fiction), but it fails to see the symbolic resonances of these names.

11. *The Turner Thesis,* ed. George Rogers Taylor (Boston: D.C. Heath, 1956), 2; hereafter cited in the text as Turner.

12. The best account of the Rothstein era is Leo Katcher's *The Big Bankroll* (New Rochelle, N.Y.: Arlington House, 1958). See especially pp. 138–48.

13. *The Letters of F. Scott Fitzgerald,* ed. Andrew Turnbull (New York: Scribner's, 1963), 551; hereafter cited in the text as *Letters.*

14. Arthur Garfield Hays, *City Lawyer* (New York: Simon & Schuster, 1942).

15. Charles Dickens, *Great Expectations* (New York: Penguin Books, 1965), 337.

16. John Keats, *English Poetry and Prose of the Romantic Movement*, ed. George B. Woods (New York: Scott, Foresman, 1950), 1357.

17. *This Side of Paradise* (New York: Scribner's, 1920), 17; *The Beautiful and the Damned* (New York: Scribner's, 1922), 126; *Tender is the Night* (New York: Scribner's, 1934), 115–17; *The Last Tycoon* (New York: Scribner's, 1941), 20.

18. Morse Peckham, "Toward a Theory of Romanticism," in *Romanticism: Points of View*, ed. Robert Gleckner and Gerald Enscoe (Englewood Cliffs, N.J.: Prentice-Hall, 1962), 217.

19. Walter Pater, *Marius the Epicurean* (New York: Modern Library, 1921), 19, 36; hereafter cited in the text as Pater.

20. Ernest Dowson, *The Poems of Ernest Dowson*, ed. Mark Longaker (Philadelphia: University of Pennsylvania Press, 1962), 146–47.

21. Henry Adams, *The Education of Henry Adams* (Boston: Houghton Mifflin, 1946), 382.

22. Interview with Marjorie King Belden, 21 February 1965.

23. Andrew Turnbull, *Scott Fitzgerald* (New York: Scribner's, 1962), 150.

24. *The Crack-Up*, 50.

25. Joan S. Korenman has pointed out the inconsistency in the color of Daisy's hair. See "'Only Her Hairdresser . . .': Another Look at Daisy Buchanan," *American Literature* 46 (January 1975): 574–78.

26. *The Apprentice Fiction of F. Scott Fitzgerald—1909–1917*, ed. John Kuehl (New Brunswick, N.J.: Rutgers University Press, 1965), 170, 172; hereafter cited in the text as *Apprentice Fiction*. Kuehl also compares George Rambert to Tom Buchanan in "A Note on the Begetting of Gatsby," *University: A Princeton Magazine*, no. 2 (Summer 1964): 26–32.

27. For the interview see Harry Salpeter, "Fitzgerald, Spenglerian," New York *World*, 3 April 1927, 12M. The short stories were part of a sequence entitled *Philippe, Count of Darkness*, which appeared in *Redbook* (October 1934, June and August 1935, and posthumously in November 1941).

28. There were nine articles on Spengler between 1922 and 1924; see the *International Index to Periodicals* and *Readers Guide to Periodical Literature*. The Stewart essay appeared in *Century* 108 (July 1924): 589–98. Dick Diver's interest in the *Century* can be found in *Tender Is the Night* (Scribner's Library edition), 211. That *The Decline of the West* was of general interest in the 1920s is suggested by Kenneth Burke's translation of the Introduction in three installments in *Dial* (November 1924 to June 1925).

29. Oswald Spengler, *The Decline of the West*, trans. Charles F. Atkinson (New York: Alfred A. Knopf, vol. 1, 1926; vol. 2, 1928), 1:21; hereafter cited in the text as Spengler.

30. Lothrop Stoddard, *Racial Realities in Europe* (New York: Scribner's, 1924), 21; hereafter cited in the text as Stoddard.

31. James R. Mellow argues that Fitzgerald was capable of his own racial prejudices: "Tom's rant is an echo of Fitzgerald's own distempered letters to Edmund Wilson about Europe and the threat of the negroid streak creeping 'northward to defile the Nordic race'" (*Invented Lives,* 221).

32. Willa Cather, *A Lost Lady* (New York: Alfred A. Knopf, 1922), 45–46; hereafter cited in the text as Cather.

33. *Correspondence,* ed. Bruccoli and Duggan, 126.

34. Ibid., 112.

35. See Keath Fraser, "Another Reading of *The Great Gatsby,*" *English Studies in Canada* 3 (Autumn 1979).

36. See Lawrence Thornton, "Ford Madox Ford and *The Great Gatsby,*" *Fitzgerald/Hemingway Annual* (Englewood, Colo.: Microcard Books, 1975), 57–74.

BIBLIOGRAPHY

Primary Works

Editions of *The Great Gatsby*

The first edition of *The Great Gatsby* appeared in April 1925; there were seven printings of that edition, including an English printing by Chatto & Windus (1926), a Modern Library printing (1934), a New Directions printing (1946), and a Grosset & Dunlap printing (1949). Since then there have been twenty-one editions of this novel, mostly by Scribner's, but also special editions by Viking, Armed Services Edition, Bantam, Dial, Grey Walls Press, Penguin, Bodley Head, and the Folio Society of London. Matthew J. Bruccoli has published an *Apparatus for F. Scott Fitzgeralds's "The Great Gatsby"* (Columbia: University of South Carolina Press, 1974), which allows for a more scholarly use of the Scribner's Library edition of 1957. Bruccoli has also published *F. Scott Fitzgerald, "The Great Gatsby": A Facsimile of the Manuscript* (Washington, D.C.: Microcard Editions Books, 1973), a photographic copy of the manuscript of *Gatsby* now held in the Princeton University Library. One can see by comparing the facsimile to the printed text, the changes, conceptual and mechanical, that Fitzgerald made in his novel. One must keep in mind, however, that as Fitzgerald worked, he recopied revised material and threw away his working papers. Thus the facsimile of the manuscript offers us remarkably clean copy at times and is not a total or true expression of Fitzgerald's revising process.

F. Scott Fitzgeralds's *Ledger* and *Notebooks*

Throughout his life, Fitzgerald kept a Ledger—a kind of occasional diary and publication record, and a Notebook, which he filled with miscellaneous observations. I have consulted both of these documents, which are among Fitzgerald's papers at Princeton University. Facsimile editions of these documents are available, however, in limited editions: *The Notebooks of F. Scott Fitzgerald*, ed. Matthew J. Bruccoli (New York: Harcourt Brace Jovanovich/Bruccoli Clark,

Bibliography

1978), and *F. Scott Fitzgerald's Ledger: A Facsimile,* introduced by Matthew Bruccoli (Washington, D.C.: Microcard Editions, 1972).

Secondary Works

Books

Callahan, John F. *The Illusions of a Nation: Myth and History in the Novels of F. Scott Fitzgerald.* Urbana: University of Illinois Press, 1972. A reading of *Gatsby* and other Fitzgerald novels in the light of the modern political climate, especially in the 1960s.

Cross, K. G. W. *Scott Fitzgerald.* New York: Capricorn Books, 1964.

Eble, Kenneth E. F. Scott Fitzgerald. New York: Twayne, 1963. One of the earliest full-length books, the revised edition appeared in 1977 (Boston: Twayne) with a brief review of Fitzgerald criticism and a "final assessment" of Fitzgerald as writer.

Gallo, Rose Adrienne. *F. Scott Fitzgerald.* New York: Frederick Ungar, 1978.

Greenfield, Howard. *F. Scott Fitzgerald.* New York: Crown, 1974.

Hindus, Milton. *F. Scott Fitzgerald: An Introduction and Interpretation.* New York: Holt, Rinehart & Winston, 1968.

Lehan, Richard. *F. Scott Fitzgerald and the Craft of Fiction.* Carbondale: Southern Illinois University Press, 1966. Treats the evolution of Fitzgeralds's fictional ideas in a context of intellectual biography; includes discussion of Fitzgerald and romantic literature, Spengler, and *The Great Gatsby* as a *roman à clef.*

Long, Robert Emmet. *The Achieving of "The Great Gatsby": F. Scott Fitzgerald, 1920–1925.* Lewisburg, Pa.: Bucknell University Press, 1979. Treats the apprentice years, the influence of Conrad, and the evolution of the manuscript.

Miller, James E., Jr. *The Fictional Technique of Scott Fitzgerald.* The Hague: Martinus Nijhoff, 1957. Revised as *F. Scott Fitzgerald: His Art and His Technique.* New York: New York University Press, 1964. Treats literary influences on Fitzgerald.

Perosa, Sergio. *The Art of F. Scott Fitzgerald.* Ann Arbor: University of Michigan Press, 1965. A critical reading of Fitzgerald's work from his Princton writings on.

Piper, Henry Dan. *F. Scott Fitzgerald: A Critical Portrait.* New York: Holt, Rinehart & Winston, 1965. Biographical criticism with emphasis upon the sources of Fitzgerald's work.

Sklar, Robert. *F. Scott Fitzgerald: The Last Laocoön*. New York: Oxford University Press, 1967. Good on background materials but argues the origin of Fitzgerald's fiction is in "the genteel romantic ideals that pervaded late nineteenth-century American culture"—a context that delimits the meaning of *The Great Gatsby*.

Stavola, Thomas J. *Scott Fitzgerald: Crisis in an American Identity*. New York: Barnes & Noble, 1979. A Jungian/Eric Erikson reading of Fitzgerald the man and his work.

Stern, Milton. *The Golden Moment: The Novels of F. Scott Fitzgerald*. Urbana: University of Illinois Press, 1970. Reads the novels as crises in an American identity.

Way, Brian. *F. Scott Fitzgerald and the Art of Social Fiction*. New York: St. Martin's Press, 1980. Sees Fitzgerald as a "successor to Edith Wharton and Henry James, both of whom brought a similar outlook and similar fictional methods to the observation of the American scene."

Whitley, J. S. *F. Scott Fitzgerald: "The Great Gatsby"*. London: Arnold, 1976. Attempts to "widen the range of reference" by connecting the novel to Keats, Conrad, Melville, and Poe.

Essay Collections

Bloom, Harold, ed. *F. Scott Fitzgerald's "The Great Gatsby."* New York: Chelsea House, 1986. Eight essays of varied approach and insight with an Introduction by Bloom placing Fitzgerald firmly within the romantic tradition.

Bruccoli, Matthew J., ed. *New Essays on "The Great Gatsby."* Cambridge: Cambridge University Press, 1985. Six essays dealing primarily with matters of theme and craft.

Donaldson, Scott, ed. *Critical Essays on F. Scott Fitzgerald's "The Great Gatsby."* Boston: G. K. Hall, 1984. Twenty-three essays, including chapters reprinted from books by Lionel Trilling, Norman Holmes Pearson, James E. Miller, Jr., Richard Lehan, and Kenneth E. Eble; and five essays written especially for this volume by Jackson R. Bryer, Alan Margolies, Ross Posnock, Robert Roulston, and Donaldson himself; material is organized around such topics as "Overview," "The Artist at Work," "Fresh Approaches," and "History-Myth-Meaning."

Eble, Kenneth E., ed. *F. Scott Fitzgerald: A Collection of Criticism*. New York: McGraw-Hill, 1973.

Hoffman, Frederick J., ed. *"The Great Gatsby": A Study*. New York: Scribner's, 1962. A collection of essays about the novel as well as useful background material such as Conrad's Preface to *The Nigger of the Narcissus*, Leo

Bibliography

Katcher's essay "The Man Who Fixed the World Series," and letters Fitzgerald wrote while working on the novel.

Kazin, Alfred, ed. *F. Scott Fitzgerald: The Man and His Work*. New York: World, 1951.

Lockridge, Ernest, ed. *Twentieth Century Interpretations of "The Great Gatsby."* Englewood Cliffs, N.J.: Prentice Hall, 1969.

Mizener, Arthur, ed. *Scott Fitzgerald: A Collection of Critical Essays*. Englewood Cliffs, N.J.: Prentice Hall, 1963.

Piper, Henry Dan, ed. *Fitzgerald's "The Great Gatsby."* New York: Scribner's, 1970.

Prigozy, Ruth, ed. F. Scott Fitzgerald Issue of *Twentieth Century Literature*, 6 (Summer 1980). Essays on *Gatsby* and other fiction and bibliographical essays by Sergio Perosa and Jackson R. Bryer.

Articles and Notes

Alderman, Taylor. *"The Great Gatsby* and *Hopalong Cassidy."* *Fitzgerald/ Hemingway Annual*. Englewood, Colo.: Microcard Books, 1975, 83–87. Believes Gatsby followed "a world in which violence and corruption have eroded the simple vision of Ben Franklin's" America.

Bruccoli, Matthew, J. " 'How Are You and the Family, Old Sport?': Gerloch and Gatsby." *Fitzgerald/Hemingway Annual*. Englewood, Colo.: Microcard Books, 1975, 33–36. "In 1923–24 when Fitzgerald was living in Great Neck he knew a man named Gerlock who employed the expression *old sport.*"

Corso, Joseph. "One Not-Forgotten Summer Night: Sources for Fictional Symbols of American Character in *The Great Gatsby."* *Fitzgerald/Hemingway Annual*. Englewood, Colo.: Microcard Books, 1976, 9–33. Believes Robert Crozier Kerr, a Great Neck neighbor of Fitzgerald's, had an experience on Sheepshead Bay in Brooklyn in 1907 similar to the one involving Gatsby saving Dan Cody's yacht.

Doyno, Victor A. "Patterns in *The Great Gatsby."* *Modern Fiction Studies* 12 (Autumn 1966):415–26. Uses holograph and galleys to see emerging stylistic patterns.

Eble, Kenneth E. "The Craft of Revision: *The Great Gatsby."* *American Literature* 36 (November 1964):315–26. One of the first genetic studies of the novel.

Gross, Dalton. "F. Scott Fitzgerald's *The Great Gatsby* and Oswald Spengler's *The Decline of the West."* *Notes and Queries* (December 1970), 467. Argues Fitzgerald may have gone to an essay by Henry de Man entitled "Germany's New Prophets" in the *Yale Review* (July 1924) for his information about Spengler.

Lehan, Richard. "F. Scott Fitzgerald and Romantic Destiny." *Twentieth Century Literature* 26 (Summer 1980):137–56. Argues for a Spenglerian reading of the canon from *Gatsby* on.

Quirk, Tom. "Fitzgerald and Cather: *The Great Gatsby.*" *American Literature* 54 (December 1982):576–91. Sees Cather's influence as all-pervasive, especially the influence of *Alexander's Bridge.*

Bibliographies

Bruccoli, Matthew J. *F. Scott Fitzgerald: A Descriptive Bibliography.* Pittsburgh: University of Pittsburgh Press, 1972; *Supplement,* 1980.

Bryer, Jackson R. *The Critical Reputation of F. Scott Fitzgerald: A Bibliographical Study.* Hamden, Conn.: Archon Books, 1967; Supplement 1 through 1981, 1984.

INDEX

Index

Index

ABOUT THE AUTHOR

Richard Lehan is a professor of English at the University of California at Los Angeles. He is the author of *F. Scott Fitzgerald and the Craft of Fiction, Theodore Dreiser: His World and His Novels,* and *A Dangerous Crossing: French Literary Existentialism and the Modern American Novel,* as well as over one hundred critical essays and literary reviews. He has held a Guggenheim Fellowship, a Fulbright Award, the University of California President's Research Fellowship, and distinguished teaching awards from the University of Texas, Austin, and UCLA. He is currently completing a book on the city in history and literature.